ICO
NIC

Shaping Visual Communication in the Digital Age

In the fast-paced digital age, where information is exchanged in bite-sized portions, the language of brands is evolving. Today, brands communicate through a blend of visual and verbal elements, reflecting the brevity of texting and social media. The modern consumer navigates a complex world using symbols, pictograms, and visual shortcuts, highlighting the ascendancy of space-efficient, time-saving, and cross-cultural symbolism over written language.

> TODAY, BRANDS COMMUNICATE THROUGH A BLEND OF VISUAL AND VERBAL ELEMENTS, REFLECTING THE BREVITY OF TEXTING AND SOCIAL MEDIA.

As we delve into an on-demand culture, visual communication emerges as the essential means of conveying messages. The design landscape, moulded by screens, has influenced not only the aesthetics of logos but also the desire for utility and purpose. Companies like Apple and Airbnb are emblematic of this shift, seeking logos that transcend mere emblems to become tools aligning with our visually driven digital interactions.

Context is paramount in communication, a fact evident in our daily activities, from scrolling through Twitter to scrutinising work reports or deciphering cereal box ingredients. Words typed into phones and keyboards are translated into computer languages, traversing the globe to appear on other screens. However, despite our reliance on written language, humans are inherently visual beings, processing visual information 60,000 times faster than text.

The roots of visual communication trace back to humanity's earliest languages, which were entirely visual. Pictograms, resembling what they signify, and ideograms, representing ideas, were universal in conveying messages. The journey of pictograms extends to road signs, where Margaret Calvert's iconic work in the UK became a cornerstone of road sign design, emphasising simplicity and clarity.

Iconography's expansion into daily life is evident in bank cards, airport signage, detergent bottles, and more. Notably, iconography plays a crucial role in globally significant events like the Olympics, using redesigned pictograms as a branding opportunity that transcends language barriers.

The digital era saw the birth of pixel art icons in the 1980s, with pioneers like Susan Kare creating iconic designs for the Apple Macintosh. Isometric design, introduced on the Atari TOS in 1985, added depth to the flat computer screen, marking a crucial point in the evolution of icon design and graphical user interface.

Skeuomorphism, championed by Steve Jobs, brought realism to digital icons, evolving into intricate lifelike representations. Subsequent years witnessed diverse design styles, from isometric icons to minimalistic and vibrant aesthetics, reflecting the dynamic nature of iconography.

No discussion of iconography is complete without acknowledging the evolution of the emoji. Originally a Japanese form of communication, emojis have become a global language, providing emotional depth and humour to digital conversations. Apple's contribution to beautifully crafted emojis and the introduction of Animoji, for example, underscore the ongoing redefinition of icons and their future potential.

Icons and pictograms serve as powerful tools for visual communication, with distinct characteristics. Icons offer artistic freedom, while pictograms demand universality and clarity. The debate over the differences between icons, pictograms, and symbols highlights their unique roles in conveying information.

Modern branding is witnessing a paradigm shift, where users, arguably, interact more with a tool than with the actual people behind a company. Brands like Uber exemplify this, where the user experience is profoundly visual, navigating through a language of sensory elements, icons, and graphics. Design elements now sit at the core of user relationships, reminiscent of a time when design faced constraints due to crude reproduction and limited space.

The on-demand age we are witnessing introduces a new visual lexicon, where symbols like Bluetooth, USB, and hashtags seem to convey meaning across generations. Familiar images, such as a cloud or a hamburger, now hold different connotations, reflecting a changing language. Designers embracing the on-demand age see screen-based visual identities not as a problem but as an opportunity to imbue character and meaning into their work.

ICONS AND PICTOGRAMS, BORN OUT OF A NEED FOR EFFICIENT COMMUNICATION, HAVE BECOME INDISPENSABLE IN SHAPING OUR DIGITAL WORLD.

Icons and pictograms, born out of a need for efficient communication, have become indispensable in shaping our digital world. They transcend language barriers, enhance productivity, and provide a visual shorthand for complex ideas. From ancient pictorial signs to modern emojis, the evolution of iconography continues to shape how we communicate, navigate, and express ourselves in the ever-evolving digital landscape. Icons are not just symbols; they are the visual language of our shared experiences, contributing to a world that is safer, more understandable, and, ultimately, more human.

PICTOGRAMS IN BRANDING

Alia és el programa del CCCB per a joves que vincula la investigació i divulgació científica amb la creació artística i literària. Alia. Les ciutats i la salut planteja sis reptes per imaginar el futur de les nostres ciutats i repensar el seu vincle amb la salut humana i planetària.

Alia. Les ciutats i la salut

Un projecte del CCCB en col·laboració amb l'Institut de Salut Global de Barcelona (ISGlobal) i el col·lectiu Mixité.

CCCB   Global   Mixité   S T·ARTS

Un projecte del Departament de Mediació del CCCB

Coordinació científica: Carolyn Daher, Natalia Rosón, Carlota Sáenz de Tejada Granados, Celia Santos Tapia, Patricia Tarín Carrasco, Marina Tarrús Batllorlló, Mònica Ubalde. Art i Comunitat. Coordinació CCCB: Raquel Morcillo Garcia. Assessoria de continguts: Celia Santos Tapia, Mixité. Territori. Disseny i maquetació: León Romero. Amb el suport i la col·laboració de l'Institut de Salut Global de Barcelona (ISGlobal) i Mixité. Territori. Art i Comunitat. Amb el suport de: STARTS (Science, Technology & the...

CCCB   Global   Mixité

6

THE COMPLEXITY OF THE INITIAL ASSIGNMENT HIGHLIGHTED THE NEED TO UNIFY FOUR FRAMEWORKS INTO A SHARED LANGUAGE AND VISUAL IDENTITY. LEÓN ROMERO DECIDED TO CREATE A UNIQUE ICONOGRAPHIC ELEMENT TO DISTINGUISH EACH OF THE FOUR BLOCKS. ●

CENTRE DE CULTURA CONTEMPORÀNIA DE BARCELONA

LEÓN ROMERO
→ leonromero.work

The Barcelona Center for Contemporary Culture, widely known as the CCCB, presented LEÓN ROMERO with the challenge of creating the identity and communication campaign for four simultaneous frameworks, each containing a number of contents and activities: Alia, Bioscopi (Bioscope), Escola en Residència (School in Residence) and Diàlegs amb Mediadors a les Exposicions (Conversations with Exhibition Mediators). These frameworks stem from the CCCB's Mediation department, an organisation that seeks to establish a dialogue between local entities, institutions and schools with the goal of making culture accessible and democratic.

The complexity of the initial assignment highlighted the need to unify four frameworks into a shared language and visual identity. LEÓN ROMERO decided to create a unique iconographic element to distinguish each of the four blocks, and by favouring image over text, set them apart from one another to make them recognisable and communicate their individual contents in a direct and highly visual way.

Xavi García, Álvaro Picca, LEÓN ROMERO

Un projecte de transformació educativa
al barri del Raval que neix de la col·laboració
l'INS Miquel Tarradell i el CCCB.

**Escola en
Residència**

CCCB

COLLEZIONE CASA MARRAZZO 1934

CASA MARRAZZO

❀ AUGE DESIGN
→ auge-design.com

Casa Marrazzo is a family-owned Italian preserves manufacturer, based in Campania since 1934. Teresa and Gerardo Marrazzo approached Auge Design with a brief to create a special range of high-quality products traditionally crafted in a new custom jar. Inspired by the company's rich heritage, they wanted it to be unique, deeply rooted and truly authentic. Auge Design named it 'Collezione Casa Marrazzo 1934', a premium range that evokes an art collection of valuable pieces.

The design company illustrated dozens of nostalgic home objects, tools and furniture pieces, in a sophisticated yet warm, naive style. The oversized objects are screen-printed with an opaque finish on clear glass, using the colour of the ingredients as a background, this unique touch adds an extra layer of authenticity and emotional connection to the product. Custom caps were designed and a wide elegant palette created to identify each product, while simple and colourful gold-printed labels were used to make the jars stand out on the shelf. ●

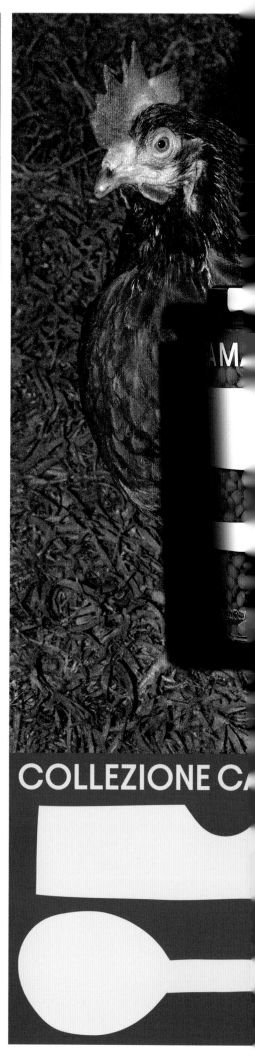

MARRAZZO 1934

COLLEZIONE CASA MARRAZZO

JUICY LUCY

✿ SOMEKIND
→ somekind.studio

Juicy Lucy is crazy about mushrooms. That's why they created the first adaptogen-infused juice in Europe. They swear by real and clean plant-based nutrition, so the juices have no artificial flavours, no refined sugars, and no preservatives. SOMEKIND designed the identity of Juicy Lucy with the personality of the brand in mind: empowered but free-spirited, driven but relaxed, ambitious but playful.

Taking age-old wisdom from traditional Chinese medicine and Ayurdevic practitioners, who use medicinal mushrooms (also known as adaptogens) to boost immunity and cure almost any ailment, they're giving it a modern twist by infusing them with a drink you can enjoy everyday. ●

◎ Buro Bonito, Martina Wunderlin

14

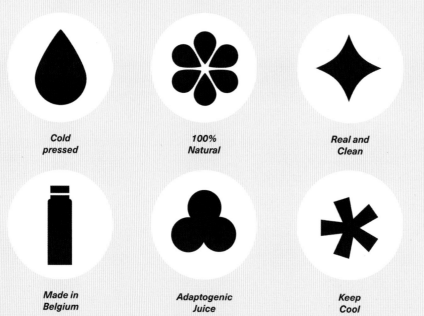

Cold pressed

100% Natural

Real and Clean

Made in Belgium

Adaptogenic Juice

Keep Cool

juicy lucy

Adaptogenic Juice

Shop   Real Talk   About

(01)

JUICY-LUCY.BE

About Us

At Juicy Lucy, we're crazy about adaptogens. That's why we created the first adaptogen-infused juice in Belgium. Made with only 100% natural ingredients, our juices are as pure as they can get.

LEARN MORE

100% Natural, Produced in Belgium, Adaptogen Infused juice

100% Natural, Produced in Belgium, Adaptogen Infused juice

SOMEKIND DESIGNED THE
IDENTITY OF JUICY LUCY WITH
THE PERSONALITY OF THE BRAND
IN MIND: EMPOWERED BUT FREE-
SPIRITED, DRIVEN BUT RELAXED,
AMBITIOUS BUT PLAYFUL. ●

BETH MIDDLETON

BETH MIDDLETON → allgood.tv

 INTERVIEW

⌨ Pictograms and icons often need to convey complex ideas in a simple visual form. How do you approach the challenge of simplification while maintaining clarity and meaning in your designs?

Making sure that the icon can stand alone without any supporting text is the real test for this. We tend to do a general Google search for images associated with the topic in mind, this generates the most obvious results which gives you a better understanding around the visuals cues associated with the topic. Not having icons that are too similar also helps distinguish the icons from each other. Understanding the audience is key, as different audiences may interpret icons differently.

⌨ How does the design of pictograms and icons differ when creating for print versus digital platforms, and what considerations do you take into account for each medium?

With digital there is the opportunity to animate, which may get across the meaning of the icon better. With animation you can get across the personality of the brand within a few seconds as opposed to print which may need the brand's tone of voice to carry that message forward. A small movement from within the icon can allow the audience to interpret it in a completely different way. With both mediums there's the limitation of accessibility and legibility.

⌨ In your experience, how do cultural differences affect the interpretation of pictograms and icons? Can you provide examples of how you've adapted your designs for different cultural contexts?

From our experience, it's key to build a strong relationship with your client to be able to adapt and avoid any cultural mistranslation, as well as strong research. One of our clients launched a barley drink that originally was brought to the UK market. After growth, the brand was launched in China which meant our current brand needed assessing to cater for the new target audience. When working on the packaging illustration, it was imperative to ensure that none of the characters could be interpreted badly. We ended up changing our ideas for two of these characters to avoid any bad connotations after some research.

⌨ Could you discuss your favourite project including pictograms or icons and the story behind it? What makes it stand out among your body of work?

The icon set we did for Oatier worked so well because it encapsulated the cheeky, vibrant personality of the brand. They also became great assets to use in sticker form, adding more visual aids into designs or just purely for decorative reasons. They also transformed into little gifs that the client could then use across their social.

⌨ Icons and pictograms can be used for various purposes, from signage to user interfaces. What are some common challenges you face in adapting your designs to different applications, and how do you address them?

Scalability and legibility are main factors as well as keeping everything consistent across each platform. Making sure icons work across multiple sizes is key. This needs to be in the forefront of your mind when crafting your icons. Thinking about the brand world and where these icons will sit and testing these visuals out early on in your process helps avoid any mishaps. In terms of scalability, not over complicating each icon helps the visual to still work on small scale as well as large.

Line thickness is also something to bear in mind. It can be the bane of many cross-channel projects and with that sometimes scaling can make these icons appear a lot chunkier than intended.

⌨ For aspiring designers looking to integrate pictogram and icon design into their work, what advice would you give them? Are there key skills or practices they should prioritise in their journey?

Firstly, it's good to think, is this aiding the design or is it adding unnecessary content? Creating a suite of icons that has a unique design quirk is always a nice nod to the brand itself. This could be brought forward in various ways. Could colour reinforce the meaning behind the icon's design? Is there a mark-making style or texture within the brand that could be enhanced? Sometimes icons can form part of a wider illustration style that can aid in telling a story. ●

☻ THE ICON SET WE DID FOR OATIER WORKED SO WELL BECAUSE IT ENCAPSULATED THE CHEEKY, VIBRANT PERSONALITY OF THE BRAND. THEY ALSO BECAME GREAT ASSETS TO USE IN STICKER FORM, ADDING MORE VISUAL AIDS INTO DESIGNS OR JUST PURELY FOR DECORATIVE REASONS. ☻

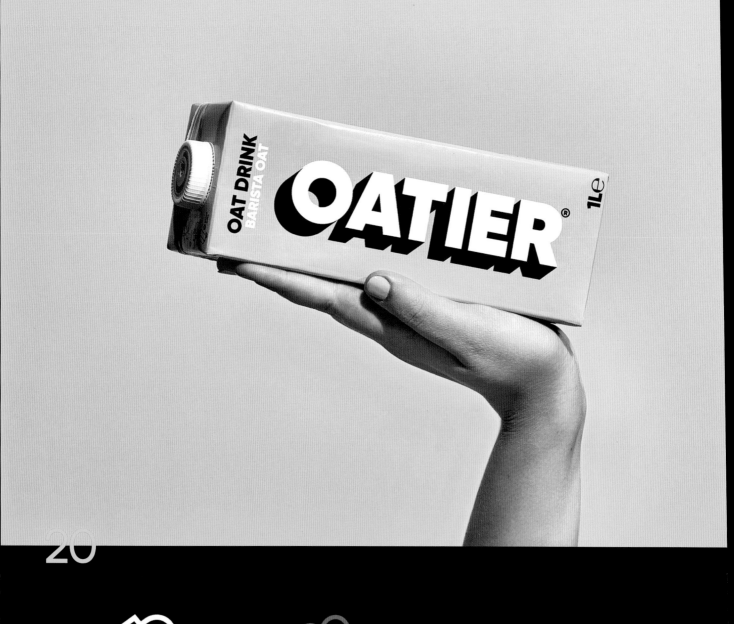

OATIER

ALLGOOD
→ allgood.tv

The Ancient Grain Company approached ALLGOOD to create a name and brand for a new oat milk that could shake up the market. ALLGOOD's branding workshop uncovered the key differentiators: their use of pure 100% Irish oats and a guaranteed frothier, tastier experience. The feedback was clear, it was a superior, oatier drink. So they called it Oatier.

Something bold had to happen for Oatier to stand out, so ALLGOOD crafted a logo and typestyle that felt like it jumped off the pack. Their team got to work writing an entire language for Oatier, something built from the name upwards. ●

LVL UP

◊ DATE OF BIRTH
→ dateofbirth.com.au

LVL UP is an electrolyte powder with great flavour and next-level hydration. It's where flavour meets function, with added vitamins and electrolytes, it packs more into your day. From tangy lime to sweet summer berry, its flavours help you re-fuel – fast.

    LVL UP isn't just a product; it's a lifestyle. DATE OF BIRTH's design embodies this, aiming to revolutionise the category and connect deeply with consumers. It captures hearts and minds, representing a brand that resonates with modern lifestyles. ●

SUPPORTS ELECTROLYTE BALANCE

RELIEVE SYMPTOMS OF DEHYDRATION

IMPROVED PHYSICAL PERFORMANCE

23

REDUCED FATIGUE & RECOVERY TIME

SUPPORTS ENERGY LEVELS

24

MARAMEO

✧ AFTER HOURS
→ afterhoursstudio.com.au

Italian restaurant Marameo is a palace of pasta, aperitivo, and rollicking good times. After Hours set out to translate this story into a visual narrative, creating a brand that is vibrant, dynamic, and filled with an invigorating energy. The name 'Marameo' itself embodies this ethos, signifying the act of thumbing one's nose.

Taking inspiration from the visionary Italian designer Depero, After Hours curated a visual language enriched with a versatile suite of iconography. This collection beautifully represents the joys of Marameo: eating and drinking, with the hand icon as a constant motif.

This hand, though consistent, serves as a canvas, capable of holding various elements like a wine glass, pasta, or fork, reflecting a diverse range of offerings. With new campaigns and offerings, the suite can be extended at any time, seamlessly integrating new elements while maintaining a cohesive and authentic representation of the brand. ●

☐ Kris Paulsen, Bendito

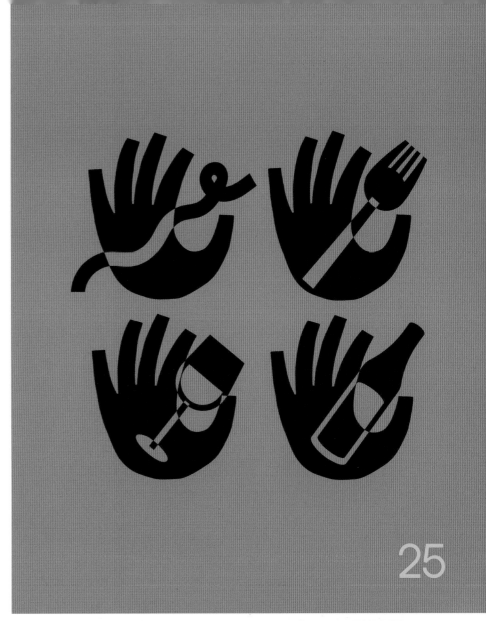

25

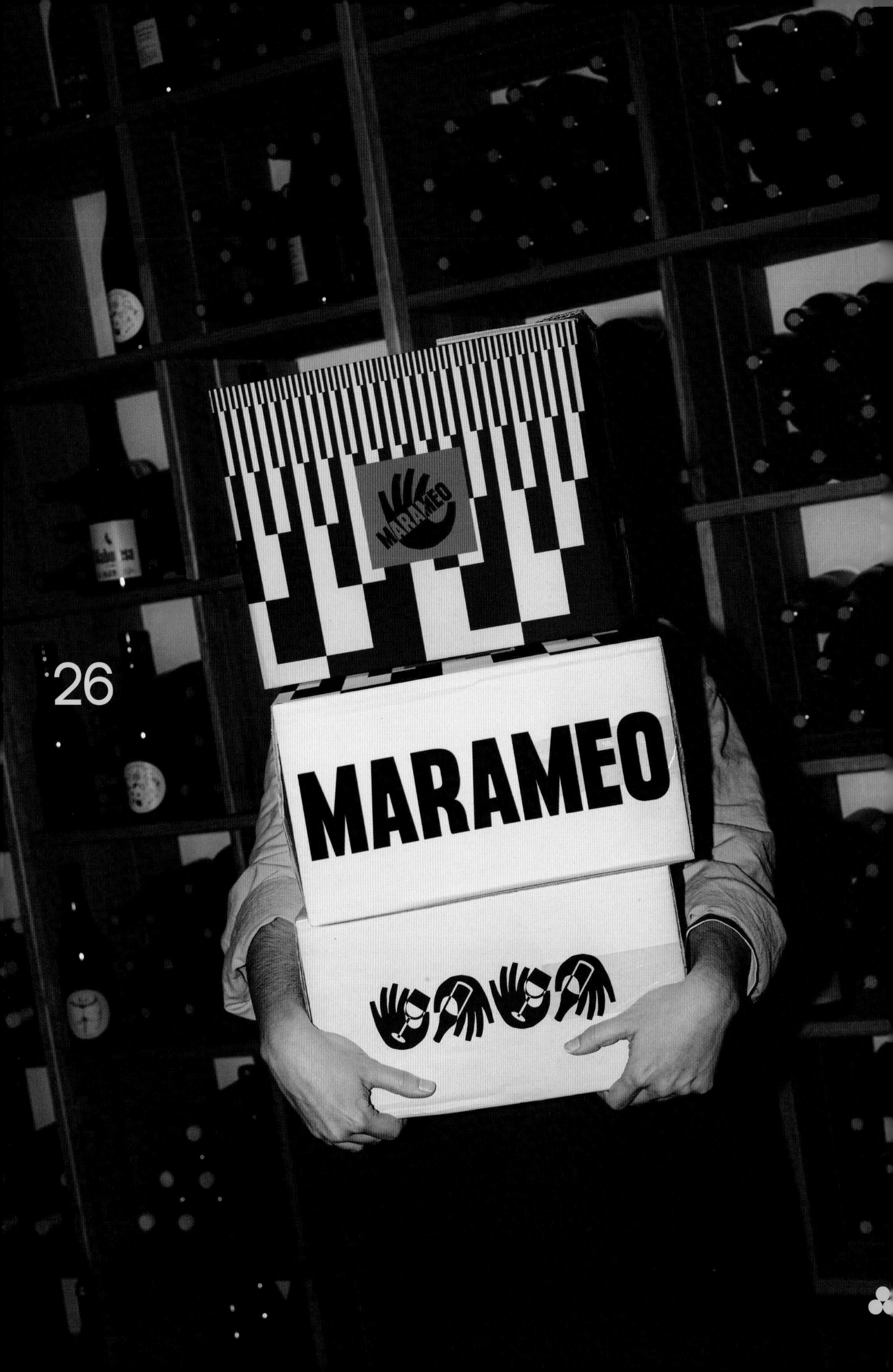
MARAMEO
MARAMEO

THIS COLLECTION BEAUTIFULLY REPRESENTS
THE JOYS OF MARAMEO: EATING AND DRINKING,
WITH THE HAND ICON AS A CONSTANT MOTIF. ●

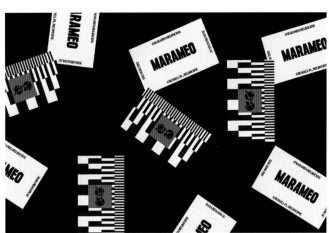

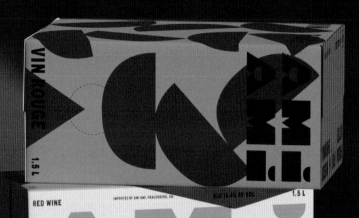

VIN ROUGE

1.5 L

RED WINE   IMPORTED BY AMI AMI, HEALDSBURG, CA.   ALC 12.4% BY VOL   1.5 L

PRODUCT OF FRANCE

GOVERNMENT WARNING: (1) ACCORDING TO THE SURGEON GENERAL, WOMEN SHOULD NOT DRINK ALCOHOLIC BEVERAGES DURING PREGNANCY BECAUSE OF THE RISK OF BIRTH DEFECTS. (2) CONSUMPTION OF ALCOHOLIC BEVERAGES IMPAIRS YOUR ABILITY TO DRIVE A CAR OR OPERATE MACHINERY, AND MAY CAUSE HEALTH PROBLEMS.

CONTAINS SULFITES

VIN ROUGE

AMI AMI

🐝 Wedge
→ wedge.work

Did you know that shipping delicious French wine in
a box (vs. a traditional bottle) over an ocean makes
50% less carbon impact?

   Ami Ami is a California-based company that thinks
outside the bottle and makes doing a little bit of good
as easy as drinking fantastic French wine.

   Wedge joined Ami Ami's co-founders Woody
Hambrecht (former co-founder Haus) & Ross Dawkins
to build the brand vision from the ground up and define
a distinct signature that invites you into a world of wine
without rules, at every touchpoint. Unfussy and friendly.
Made to enjoy how you want to. Eye-catching on shelf,
online, and on your table. Making the box a thing of desire. ●

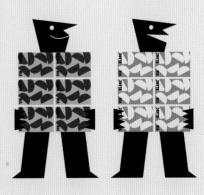

WHITE WINE   IMPORTED BY AMI AMI, HEALDSBURG, CA.   ALC 12.3% BY VOL   1.5 L

PRODUCT OF FRANCE

GOVERNMENT WARNING: (1) ACCORDING TO THE SURGEON GENERAL, WOMEN SHOULD NOT DRINK ALCOHOLIC BEVERAGES DURING PREGNANCY BECAUSE OF THE RISK OF BIRTH DEFECTS. (2) CONSUMPTION OF ALCOHOLIC BEVERAGES IMPAIRS YOUR ABILITY TO DRIVE A CAR OR OPERATE MACHINERY, AND MAY CAUSE HEALTH PROBLEMS.   **CONTAINS SULFITES**

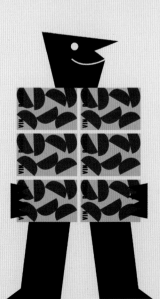

GOGO

⌘ MEAT
→ meat.studio

'gogo' is a fast food and convenience store brand created by the Beijing Subway.

An 8×8 pixel grid is used to represent food offerings as videogame-themed icons, like high-fives to everyone making it through their commute. There's nostalgia and humour to the unrealistically chunky icons.

The gogo wordmark incorporates 'cut corners' at the joints of strokes of both Latin and Chinese type. The pixelated icon and typographic approach speak to the store's online order and in-store pickup options.

Inspired by 8-bit era gaming, the colour scheme leverages the digital aesthetic by maximising colour saturation while retaining warmth and friendliness. ●

THE PIXELATED ICON AND TYPOGRAPHY APPROACH SPEAK TO THE STORE'S ONLINE ORDER AND IN-STORE PICKUP OPTIONS. ●

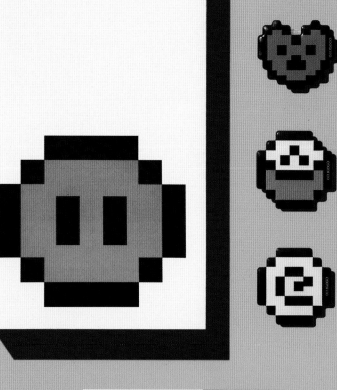

gogo DELIGOGO 桃气十足——→ 白桃乌龙蛋糕卷 gogo

gogo DELIGOGO 粒粒皆不同 →军舰寿司 gogo

gogo DELIGOGO 怪(善)的——→ 大满贵沙拉BOWL go

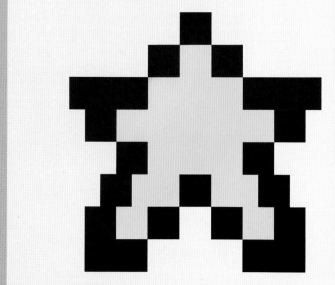

gogo DELIGOGO 金饭碗——→ 红咖喱华肉饭

gogo DELIGOGO 内心(澎湃)——→ 黑巧克力熔岩蛋糕

gogo DELIGOGO 停留(片)刻→ ——→枫糖吐司

gogo DELIGOGO 日日燃→日日清 ——→杏仁牛角包

gogo
DELIGOGO

MOUNTAIN CLUB

MAKEBARDO
→ makebardo.com

The Mountain Club company is more than just a coworking space business – they also run the Beach Street Cafe, where you can start your day with the unique Mountain Club vibes. Therefore, it was crucial for MAKEBARDO to establish a consistent and flexible visual identity that could represent both entities.

They created a shield-style logo that symbolises teamwork and belonging and used it as a basis to develop a set of personal icons. The cup icon, which serves as the pictorial mark of the cafe, was also derived from these shapes. To reinforce the brand's identity, MAKEBARDO used typefaces that emit strength and solidity, which a well-known type designer, René Bieder, created.

Additionally, they created a set of wayfinding pictograms, separate from the primary icons' aesthetics, to provide more assets for the identity. The result is a cohesive, attractive, and versatile brand identity. ●

Kate Roberge, Emile Hussell

85 Beach Street
Lakeside espresso bar in
the heart of Queenstown.

Open Monday — Friday
7:30am to 4pm

Great coffee, chats &
treats.

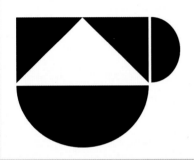

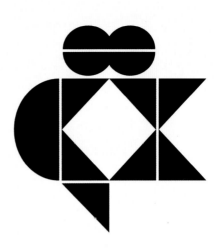

Workshops

Our spaces are designed to empower
collaboration or focus. We add the detail,
allowing you to invest your time with us to
plan, create, motivate, or persuade.

Events &
Experiences.

85 Beach Street
Lakeside espresso bar in
the heart of Queenstown.

Open Monday — Friday
7:30am to 4pm

Great coffee, chats &
treats.

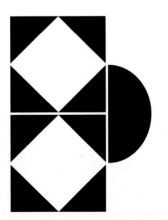

Curate events & experiences
to drive motivation and
connection.

Make an impact with your
event. Our team tailor-make
every experience to the
interests and goals of your
stay. We'll take care of it all,
from business conferences
to workshops.

Workspaces

Enjoy a dynamic
and collaborative
workplace for any
interaction.

Our Workspace plans are available for members only and we cater to everyone's needs, from
individuals to companies. We curate community events for our members during the year,
from our much-loved conversation series to wellness workshops, biking, hiking and skiing.

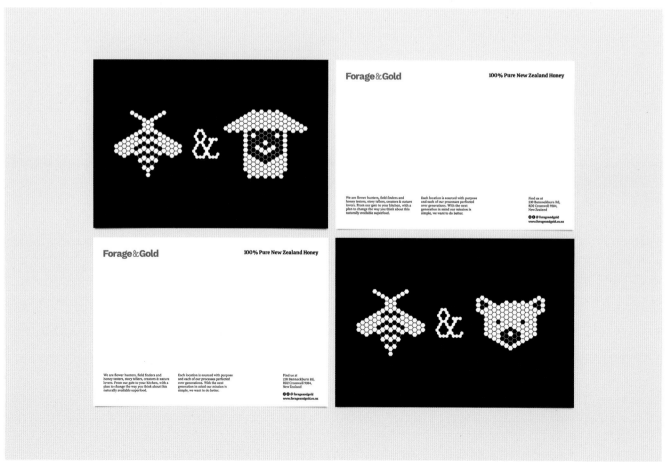

FORAGE & GOLD

⊗ MAKEBARDO
→ makebardo.com

Forage & Gold has been created with the next generation in mind. Packaged in glass jars, with the same great taste and the option to return your packaging for re-use. They want to create a honey company that has as little impact as possible while delivering delicious honey, and providing ideas and suggestions for everyday use.

For the visual identity, MAKEBARDO were inspired by the essential elements of this category. The hexagonal pattern of a honeycomb's morphology fascinated them, and they were excited to experiment with the open and capped honey cells to create a visually appealing graphic outcome.

Forage & Gold's brand identity stands out in this highly competitive category with its simple and powerful visual language. The design exudes a vibrant, reliable, and fun personality that resonates with the audience.

The label design is straightforward yet coherent throughout the product range, making it easy to create future products. In contrast, using a triple side label for different display options gives the brand a unique edge. ●

📷 Julia Gray

THE DESIGN EXUDES A VIBRANT, RELIABLE, AND FUN PERSONALITY THAT RESONATES WITH THE AUDIENCE. ● 39

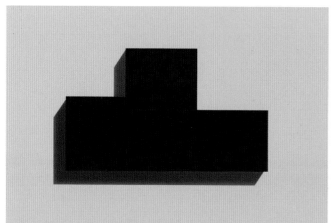

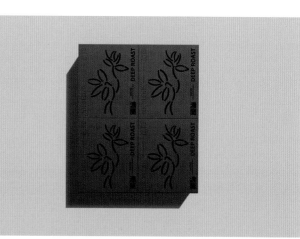

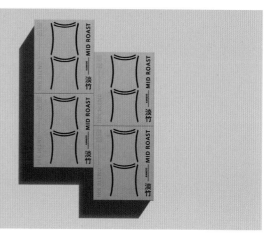

INK BLEND

🖾 LUNG-HAO CHIANG
→ behance.net/st60701

In Chinese ink painting, there's the concept of 'Five Shades of Ink', representing the five variations of black from intense to subtle ¦dark, rich, heavy, light, and clear¦. Drawing inspiration from this, LUNG-HAO CHIANG blended the floral themes of ink painting, typically plum, orchid, bamboo, chrysanthemum, and pine, with the roasting levels and flavours of coffee.

Ink painting focuses on conveying an atmosphere, leaving room for imagination, emphasising essence over detail with significant whitespace. The process is referred to as 'writing', not 'painting'. ●

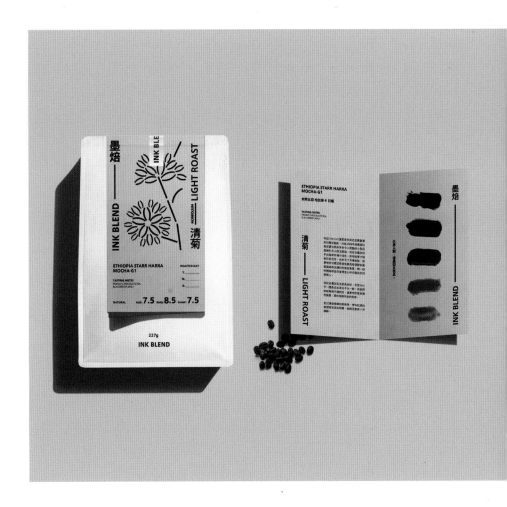

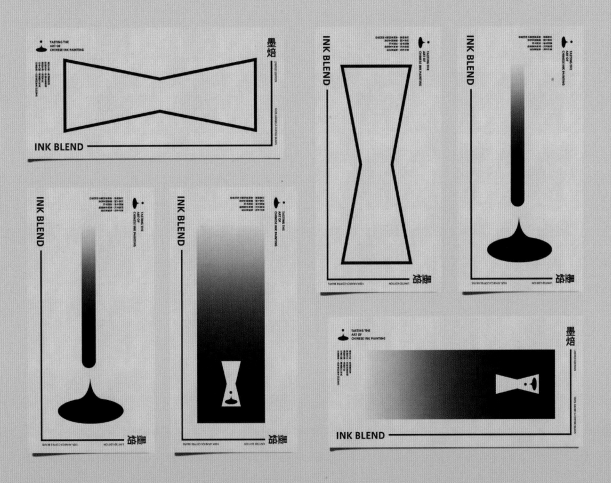

⚠RETURN TO NATURE, EXPLORE THE PURE. BE COMMITTED TO ORIGINAL(原创的) DESIGN AND ADVOCATE (无公式)NO-FORMULA WEAR⬆, MADE BY NATURE🌐, DESIGN BY ⑤SENDAWAY. CHECK THE CERTIFICATE(合格证) ON THE BACK. COPYRIGHT ©2022 SENDAWAY. ALL RIGHTS RESERVED.

SENDaWay.

⚠RETURN TO NATURE, EXPLORE THE PURE. BE COMMITTED TO (原创的) ORIGINAL DESIGN AND ADVOCATE (无公式)NO-FORMULA WEAR⬆, MADE BY NATURE🌐, DESIGN BY SENDaWay®. DON'T LITTER🗑 THE ⑤BUBBLE BAG(气泡袋) FOR THE ENVIRONMENT (保护环境) AND WASH YOUR HANDS✋ IN TIME. COPY-RIGHT ©2022 SENDAWAY. ALL RIGHTS RESERVED.

⚠RETURN TO NATURE, EXPLORE THE PURE. BE COMMITTED TO (原创的)ORIGINAL DESIGN AND ADVOCATE (无公式)NO FORMULA WEAR⬆, MADE BY NATURE🌐, DESIGN BY SENDaWay. DON'T LITTER🗑 THE ㊿ EXPRESS BOX(飞机盒) FOR THE ENVIRONMENT(保护环境) AND WASH YOUR HANDS✋ IN TIME. COPYRIGHT ©2022 SENDAWAY. ALL RIGHTS RESERVED.

SENDaWay.

SENDaWay.

⚠THIS IS A UNIVERSAL ⚠TAPE(胶带). MADE BY NATURE🌐, DESIGN BY ⑤SENDAWAY. COPYRIGHT ©2022 SENDAWAY. ALL RIGHTS RESERVED.

SENDaWay.

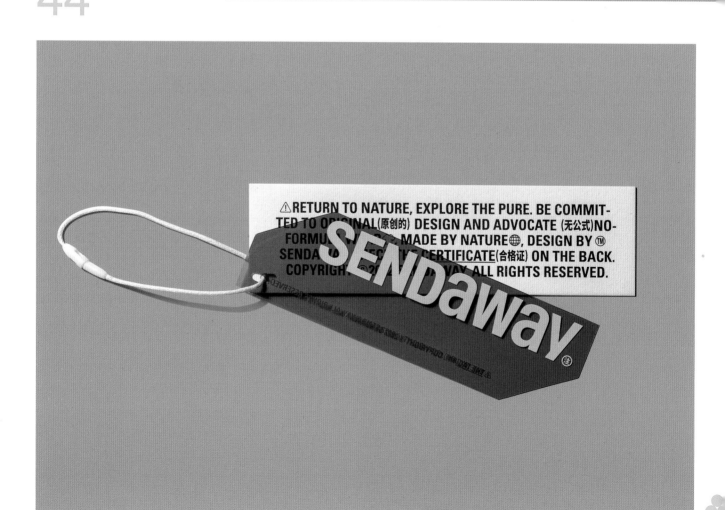

SENDAWAY

HDU²³ LAB
→ hdu23lab.com

Sendaway is a 'city-boy style' clothing brand that advocates natural, pure, loose and casual wear.

The brand identity design uses a random arrangement of text and wash icons to express the idea of 'no-formula wear'. The dense text paragraphs are a visual metaphor for the high-gram weight of the product fabrics.

SENDAWAY.

⚠️RETURN TO NATURE, EXPLORE THE PURE. BE COMMITTED TO ORIG ADVOCATE (无公式)NO FORM MADE BY NATURE🌐, DESIGN B YOU CAN ♻️REUSE THIS PLASTIC OR PLEASE TAKE CARE🗑️ OF OUR *MENT*(保护环境), COPYRIGHT © SENDAWAY. ALL RIGHTS RESERVED.

⚠️RETURN TO NATURE, EXPLORE THE PURE. BE COMMITTED TO (原创的)ORIGINAL DESIGN AND ADVOCATE (无公式)NO FORMULA WEAR👕, MADE BY NATURE🌐, DESIGN BY SENDAWAY. DON'T LITTER🗑️ THE 纸 EXPRESS BOX(飞机盒) FOR THE ENVIRONMENT(保护环境) AND WASH YOUR HANDS✋ IN TIME. COPYRIGHT ©2022 SENDAWAY. ALL RIGHTS RESERVED.

⚠RETURN TO NATURE, EXPLORE THE PURE. BE COMMITTED TO (原创的) ORIGINAL DESIGN AND ADVOCATE (无公式) NO-FORMULA WEAR👕, MADE BY NATURE🌐, DESIGN BY SENDAWAY®. DON'T LITTER🗑 THE ♲BUBBLE BAG(气泡袋) FOR THE ENVIRONMENT (保护环境) AND WASH YOUR HANDS✋ IN TIME. COPY-RIGHT ©2022 SENDAWAY. ALL RIGHTS RESERVED.

SENDaWay®

MOUNTAIN HARDWEAR

JUSTIN AU
→ justin5au.com

Founded in 1993, Mountain Hardwear gained credibility for gear engineered with supreme technicality and practicality. Justin Au created a visual identity off of a single idea, 'Wildly Engineered'.

The brand's signature nut symbol is a juxtaposition of sharp outer edges with soft internal forms – a visual metaphor for precise engineering combined with a wild human touch. The design system comes to life with an intelligent, yet expressive language. A set of icons accompanies the typeface, sharing the same geometry and weight, which convey the garment's technical engineering and ensure visual consistency across utilitarian settings.

Justin Au also developed a custom typeface called 'Hardwear' and a modular set of graphic elements for the identity.

AMOS SPORT
BUSINESS SCHOOL

ᵔ ZOO
→ z-o-o.fr

This global redesign and graphic identity by ZOO is
for a business school specialising in sports, which has
12 campuses in Europe.

ZOO developed an exclusive typeface, as well as a
set of adapted and dynamic communication tools. Their
challenge was to impart an institutional and dynamic tone,
in the service of an approach focused on the international
scene and the major sporting challenges the world will
face in the future. ●

EX
PLORE
AR
OUND
YOU

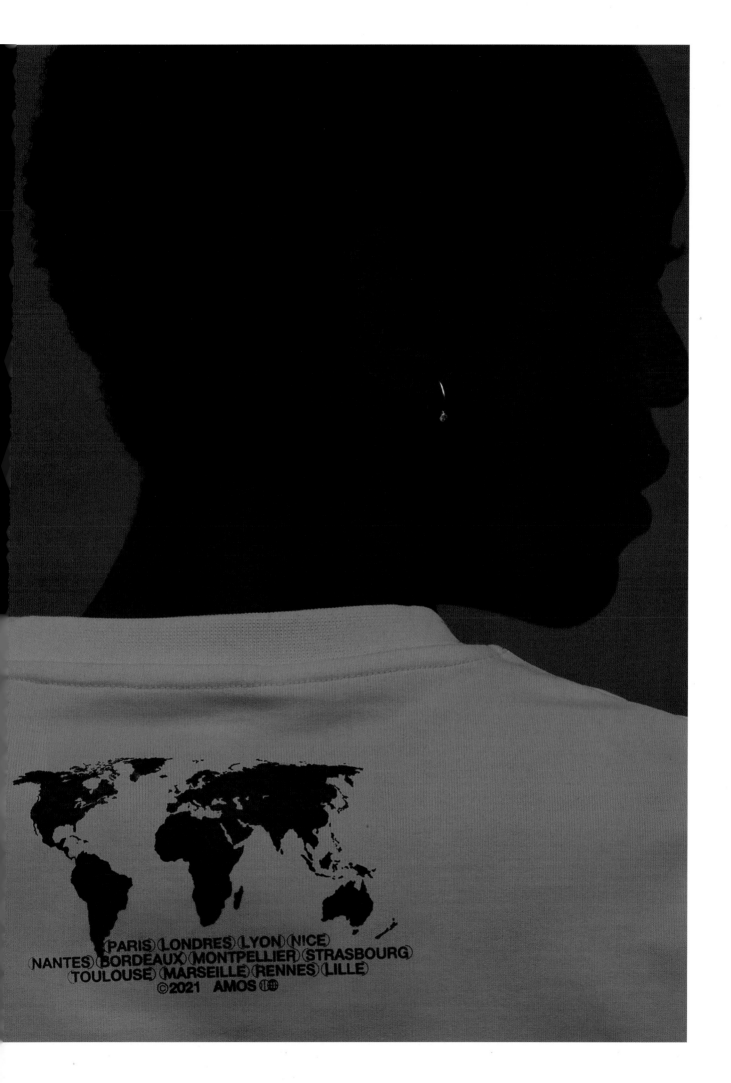

(PARIS) LONDRES) LYON) NICE)
NANTES) BORDEAUX) MONTPELLIER) STRASBOURG)
TOULOUSE) MARSEILLE) RENNES) LILLE)
©2021   AMOS ⑩

MODE

⌂ JUSTIN AU
→ justin5au.com

Led by visionary founders who created the platform believing in the universal power of data, Mode was set to build upon its success within the business intelligence space by making it accessible to a wider range of users in modern data-driven organisations.

Shifting modes is the core behaviour of the identity system: A dynamic logo and an expressive variable typeface (WT Zaft[2] by WiseType) inverts counterforms and adapts to every canvas, an analogous palette of electric greens and a graphic language of modular blocks. All these modular tools allow Mode to quickly switch from exploratory to analytical expressions, paving the way for every mode of working. ●

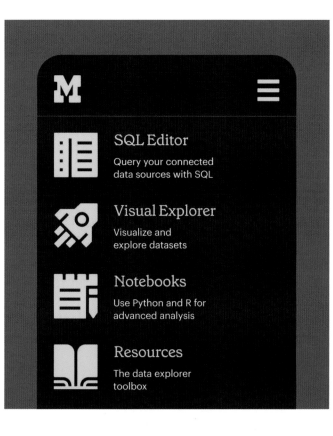

SQL Editor
Query your connected data sources with SQL

Visual Explorer
Visualize and explore datasets

Notebooks
Use Python and R for advanced analysis

Resources
The data explorer toolbox

Let's shift the way we work with data

Get in the Mode

Never get lost in your data again.

The modern data stack

Q & A

From question

To insight

56

HOMA

Ⓐ RAGGED EDGE
→ raggededge.com

With 200 people from 34 countries, 1 billion downloads of their games, and a total of $165m in funding, Homa came to Ragged Edge at an inflection point. They wanted to step up their mission to redefine the gaming industry. To succeed they needed to position themselves as an ally for independent game developers. To build a talent brand that would attract the world's best engineers. And to transform millions of gamers from fans of Homa's games, to fans of Homa itself.

Working across every part of the rapidly-expanding company, from the founding team to new joiners, Ragged Edge re-engineered their brand from the inside out. Framing Homa as a precision-tooled gaming lab, and the Homa team as its elite technicians.

For the identity Ragged Edge built a data-fuelled wonderland. A world where Homa characters can roam and developers can game the system. A framework for their ever-expanding SDK, characters, and the games themselves, realised across an ever-growing range of technologies, from mobile to web3. All delivered across a range of touchpoints, including homagames.com. ●

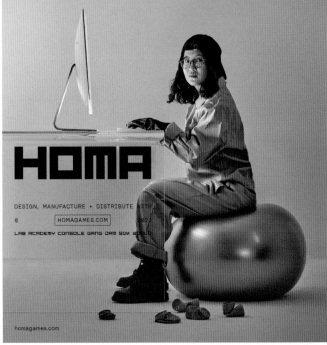

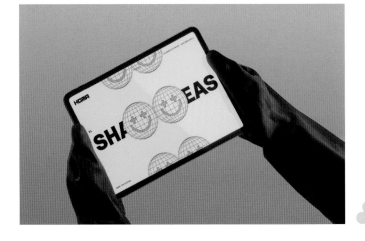

FOR THE IDENTITY RAGGED EDGE BUILT A DATA-FUELLED
WONDERLAND. A WORLD WHERE HOMA CHARACTERS CAN
ROAM AND DEVELOPERS CAN GAME THE SYSTEM. ●

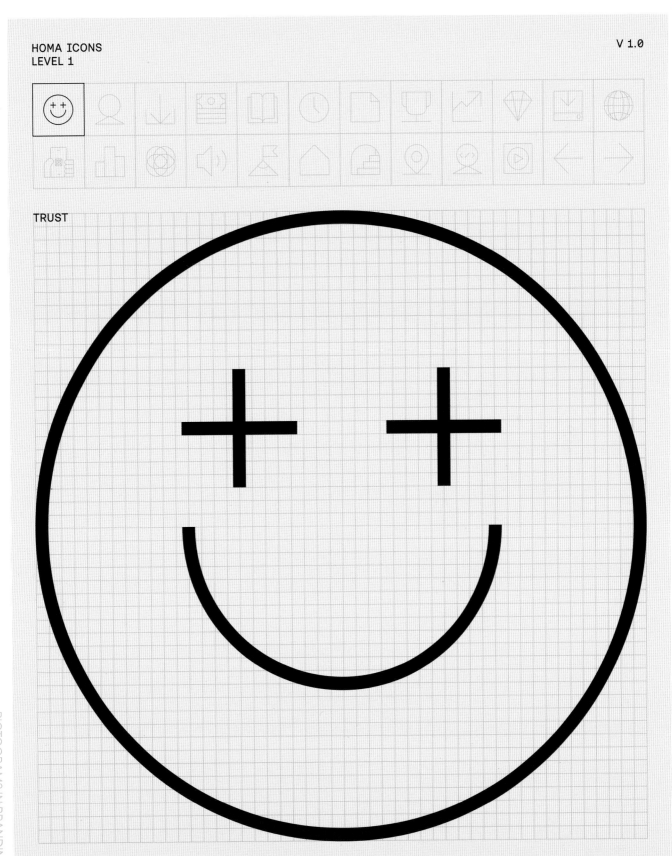

HOMA ICONS
LEVEL 1

TRUST

YEAR OF THE PIG

⌂ Lung-Hao Chiang
→ behance.net/st60701

The traditional Chinese New Year imagery is often associated with opulence and vibrant visuals. While this style is timeless, it can sometimes feel a bit stale with overexposure.

Lung-Hao Chiang aspired to offer a fresh perspective of the Spring Festival, a breezy and cheerful beginning for the new year. Drawing inspiration from greeting cards, Lung-Hao Chiang used punctuation marks exclusively to craft a Chinese New Year card that interprets contemporary aesthetics. ●

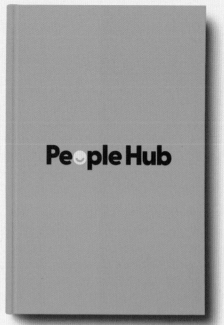

PEOPLE HUB

ALLGOOD
→ allgood.tv

People Hub are the people specialists. They approached ALLGOOD to completely rethink their brand, business model and approach.

Organisations tend to have a business plan, but what about a people plan? This is the core question ALLGOOD posed in the brand, helping to establish a story to build on.

They decided to strip everything back and centre the brand around a single fresh green colour, this helped solidify the offering and created a bold new look for the company. The striking new graphics were carried through a series of illustrations, icons and videos helping to explain the services and 'hubs'.

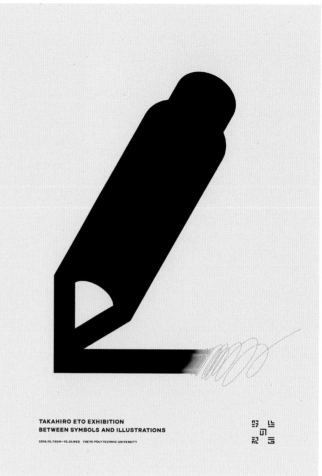

BETWEEN SYMBOLS
AND ILLUSTRATIONS

🔒 STUDY LLC. / TAKAHIRO ETO
→ studyllc.tokyo

In the process of designing pictograms and other symbols, delicate details and three-dimensionality of motifs are omitted. In this poster, these lost elements are revived, and delicacy and clarity cohabit in a single symbol. It is an attempt to give a small 'life' to a static symbol.

Originally, a symbol is a tool to convey something, but in this work, the symbol is liberated from the tool-like treatment and expresses the autonomous behaviour of the symbol itself. ●

TAKAHIRO ETO EXHIBITION
BETWEEN SYMBOLS AND ILLUSTRATIONS

2018.10.7SUN–10.24WED   TOKYO POLYTECHNIC UNIVERSITY

63

STOLP

FCKLCK STUDIO
→ fcklck.studio

Stolp is a Belgian startup that was
founded in 2020 with the purpose
of helping individuals to overcome
negative digital habits and adopt
a healthier and less phone-centric
lifestyle. The brand uses pictograms
and wayfinding to keep its messaging
easy to understand, unobtrusive, and
simple. This involves combining short,
clear lines of text with pictograms
and icons. This system brings both
rest and calm, and also draws the
necessary attention without being
overly complex. ●

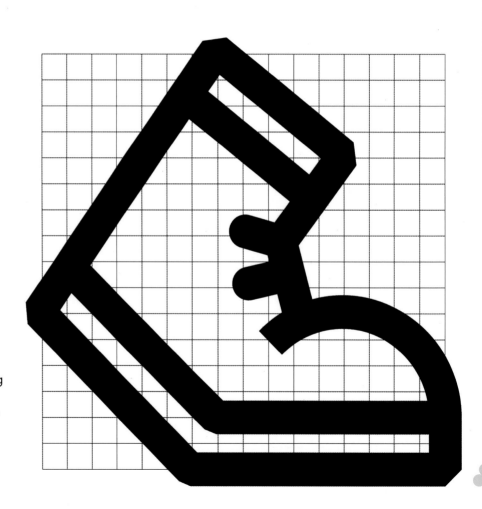

THE BRAND USES WAYFINDING TO KEEP ITS MESSAGING EASY TO UNDERSTAND, UNOBTRUSIVE, AND SIMPLE. THIS INVOLVES COMBINING SHORT, CLEAR LINES OF TEXT WITH PICTOGRAMS AND ICONS. THIS SYSTEM BRINGS BOTH REST AND CALM, AND ALSO DRAWS THE NECESSARY ATTENTION WITHOUT BEING OVERLY COMPLEX. ●

NONE

⊕ LARSSEN AMARAL
→ larssenamaral.no

'None' is an energy management
system connecting hardware to
software to help customers cut costs
and carbon emissions. The concept
for the identity is based on the visual
language from technical schematics
engineers use to map energy use.

The dynamic logo lies at
the core of the visual identity, with
various changing combinations of
symbols and pictograms representing
different types of energy sources,
junction points and distribution
networks. None's brand messaging
also mirrors these aesthetics,
supported by a custom set of icons
and patterns that expand on the
use of these monolinear symbols
to create a holistic visual narrative
truly unique to None. ●

BRILLIANT

⚘ THE STUDIO
→ the-studio.se

When Netsurvey, a leading employee engagement consultancy in Sweden, acquired Bright, experts in customer surveys, the first thing they asked The Studio to help them with was a name for the new company. After a thorough research and analysis process, the name they arrived at was 'Brilliant'. Their next task was to create a brand platform that would encapsulate the common denominators of both cultures, and that people from both organisations could identify with and stand behind. An overarching theme for the description of the value base of the new company was summarised as 'Serious Playfulness', which guided the work.

With this as a base, The Studio developed a graphic identity that bursts with vivid colours, bold and friendly typography, lively animations and a pictogram set comprising more than 50 unique icons. It is fun, warm, welcoming – but has a serious undertone, and is never gimmicky or silly. It was instantly loved by staff and customers alike and provided the perfect start for the Bright/Netsurvey marriage. ●

📷 Patrik Lindell

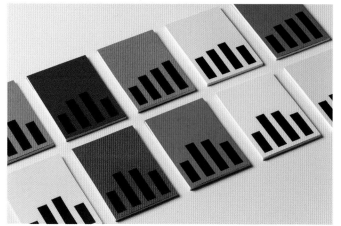

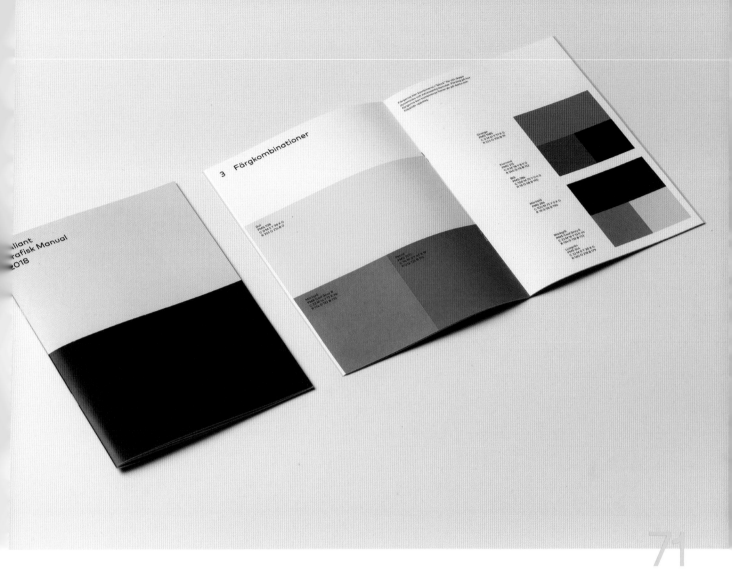

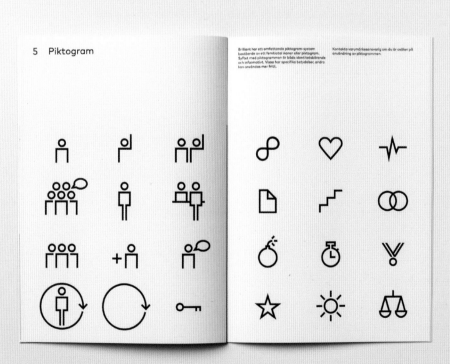

MAXIO

⊗ ORDER
→ order.design

Maxio is a subscription billing management platform designed to empower growing B2B SaaS teams and enable efficiency in their work-flow. Following the company's merger of Chargify and SaaSOptics, Order created an identity designed to balance the mathematical and human nature of the team's practice.

A custom-drawn logotype mirrors the construction of the symbol, and reinforces the data-focused practice in the unconventional letter 'X'. The symbol is used as a shorthand identifier of the brand. ●

ORDER CREATED AN IDENTITY DESIGNED TO BALANCE
THE MATHEMATICAL AND HUMAN NATURE OF THE
TEAM'S PRACTICE. ●

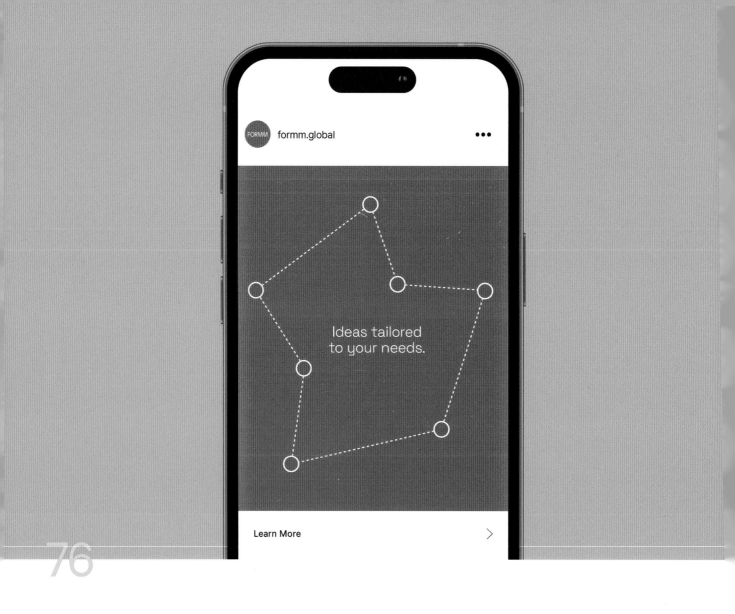

FORMM

⊖ MICHELE VERZE
→ micheleverze.com

Michele Verze created this idenity for Chasm Digital, an established consultancy and venture studio based in Australia, who were looking to scale up their services globally.

A complete toolkit, with a bold name and logo, an energetic palette and a series of exciting symbols to showcase smart thinking and freshness of approach in a simple and effective way was created.

The letter 'O' in the logo was the inspiration for the circle as a flexible brand element. This shape began to be used to capture ideas, frame images or highlight relevant content.

A series of symbols were also uniquely drawn, as an extension of the brand narrative. They helped FORMM's team convey complex ideas and business concepts in a simple and engaging way. ●

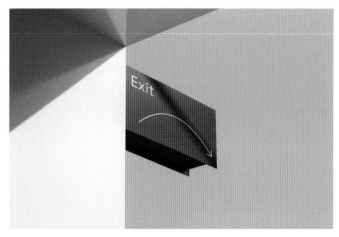

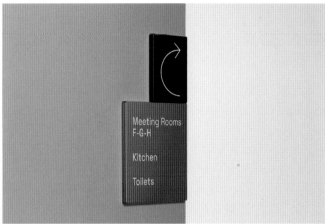

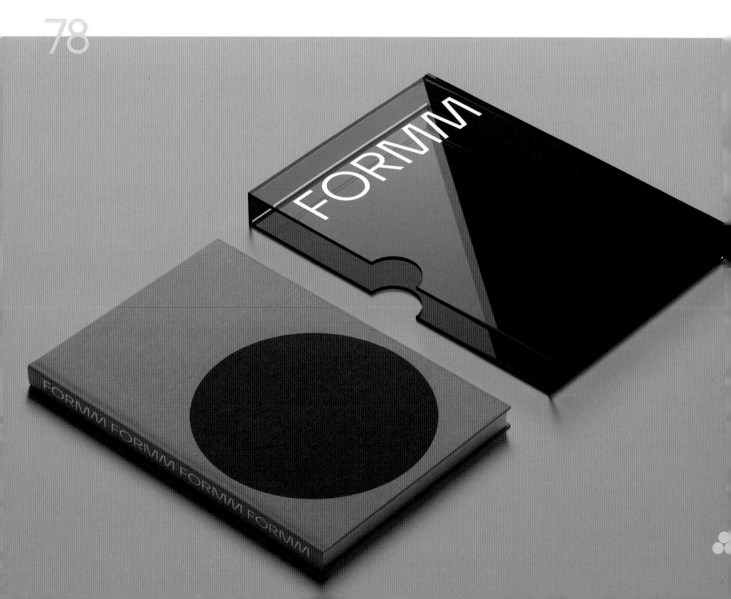

INDUSTRIOUS LABS

ORDER
→ order.design

Heavy industry is the foundation of modern society. Materials like cement, steel, and aluminium build our bridges and roads, construct wind and solar projects, and manufacture vehicles and heat pumps.

     Industrious Labs works to ensure these solutions are delivered with the environment in mind. Paying attention to the vastly different audiences, between environmental activists and industry stakeholders, the identity system highlights the power of community and collaboration.

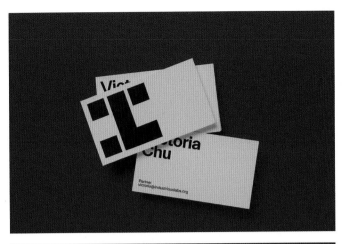

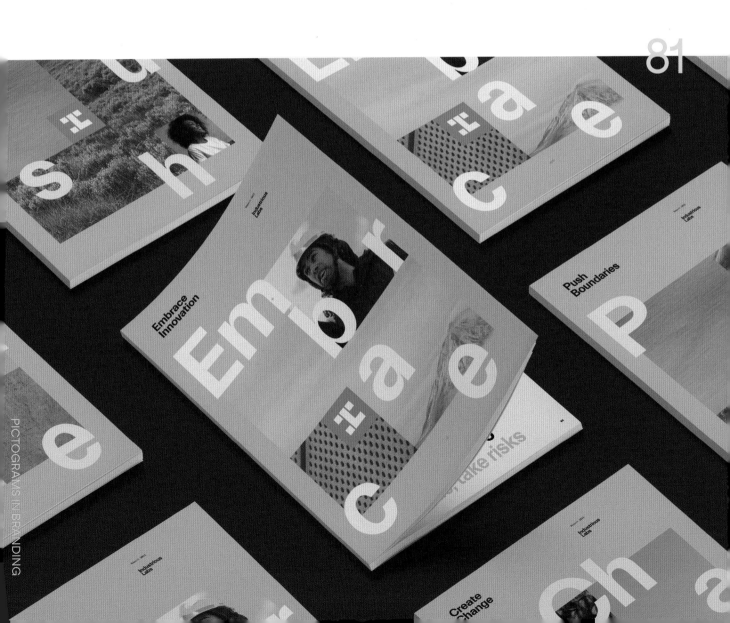

OFF-BIENNALE

⊛ CLASSMATE
→ classmatestudio.com

OFF-Biennale Budapest is the largest contemporary art event in Hungary. OFF's mission is to strengthen the local independent art scene, and initiate public discourse about urgent, yet neglected, social, political, and environmental issues.

CLASSMATE created their annual in 2021 with the theme 'Inhale', taking the seminal political poem 'A Breath of Air!' by 20th-century Hungarian poet Attila József as its starting point. In their 21st-century reading of the poem, a 'breath of air' refers simultaneously to the galloping climate catastrophe and to the threat posed on civil liberties by populist regimes and global capital alike. 'Fresh air' is also a symbol of freedom – it can refer to a site or situation in which it is possible to breathe freely.

The identity manifests a symbolic thirst for air with its vivid colour palette, energetic layouts and a set of symbolic icons to communicate the theme's versatile messages across the brand. ●

THE IDENTITY MANIFESTS
A SYMBOLIC THIRST FOR
AIR WITH ITS VIVID COLOUR
PALETTE, ENERGETIC
LAYOUTS AND A SET
OF SYMBOLIC ICONS TO
COMMUNICATE THE THEME'S
VERSATILE MESSAGES
ACROSS THE BRAND. ●

PERKSY

⎯ JUSTIN AU
→ justin5au.com

Perksy is a consumer insights platform that powers real-time research. Users play on its immersive mobile app that rewards them for answering gamified question 'stacks'. Meanwhile, brands gain real and genuine feedback.

Perksy came to Justin Au to help them define their unique position in the industry. With its primarily Millenial and Gen-Z users in mind, an expressive brand identity was created that introduces a cheeky and irreverent, yet raw and honest, voice.

At the identity's core is a visual toolkit that can emotionally react to anything and everything. Justin Au championed an expressive 'P.moji' in the brand's logomark. Inspired by the tactility of pasting stickers, a system was developed where every visual element can be stacked to create digital and physical moments that tell the unique stories behind every user. ●

84

AT THE IDENTITY'S CORE IS A VISUAL TOOLKIT THAT CAN EMOTIONALLY REACT TO ANYTHING AND EVERYTHING. ●

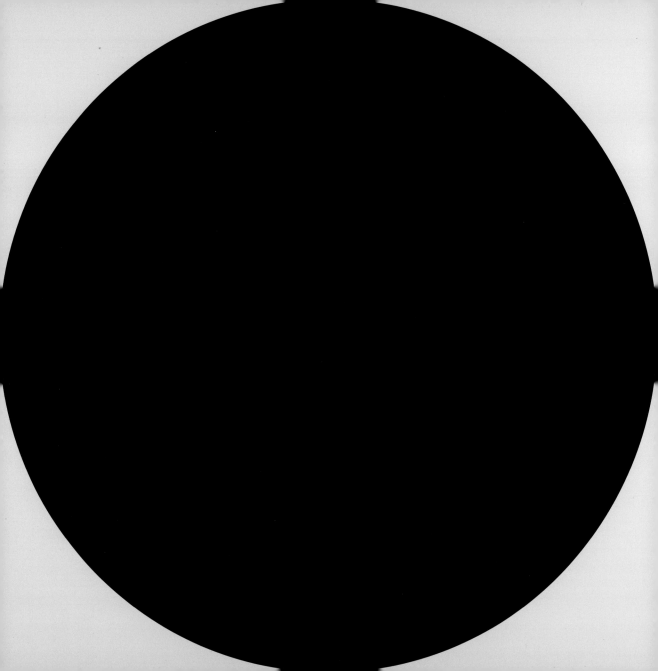

ÖTHĚRHUMAN

DUANE DALTON
→ duanedalton.com

ÖthěrHuman is a self initiated design project initially
created to showcase a typeface in use, FT Polar by Frost
Type. It was then further developed with a focus on mascot
creation using iconography, systematic principles and
playfulness. The goal was to distil various human stances
and positions down to their simplest forms. The result is
an outcome that has been applied across various touchpoints including print, 3D, embroidered patches and
signage to demonstrate the full effect of the identity.

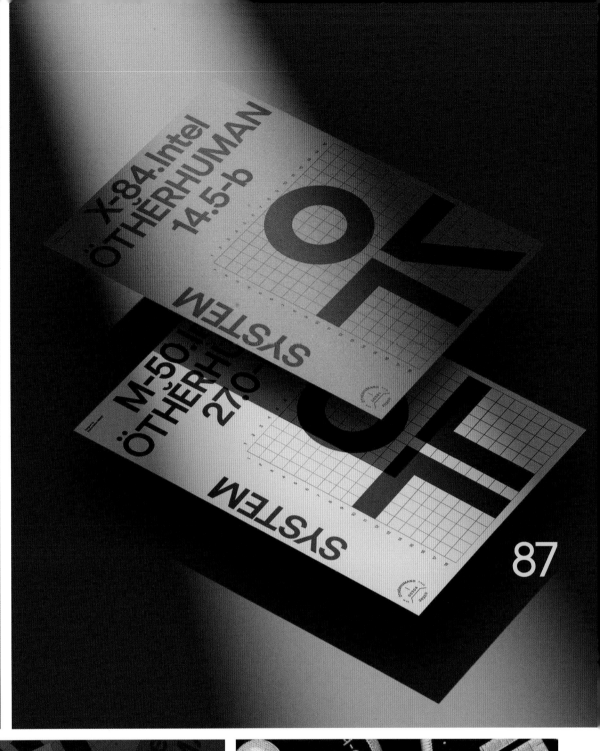

X-84.Intel
ÖTHĔRHUMAN
14.5-b

SYSTEM

M-50.Intel
ÖTHĔRHUMAN
27.0-b

SYSTEM

G-82.Intel
ÖTHĔRHUMAN
24.0-b

G-12.Intel
ÖTHĔRHUMAN
18.5-b

ÖTHĔRHUMAN©
Ö.H.[FOUR]
27.0-b

Endlĕssly Evölving.

ŌthĕrHuman

otherhuman.com

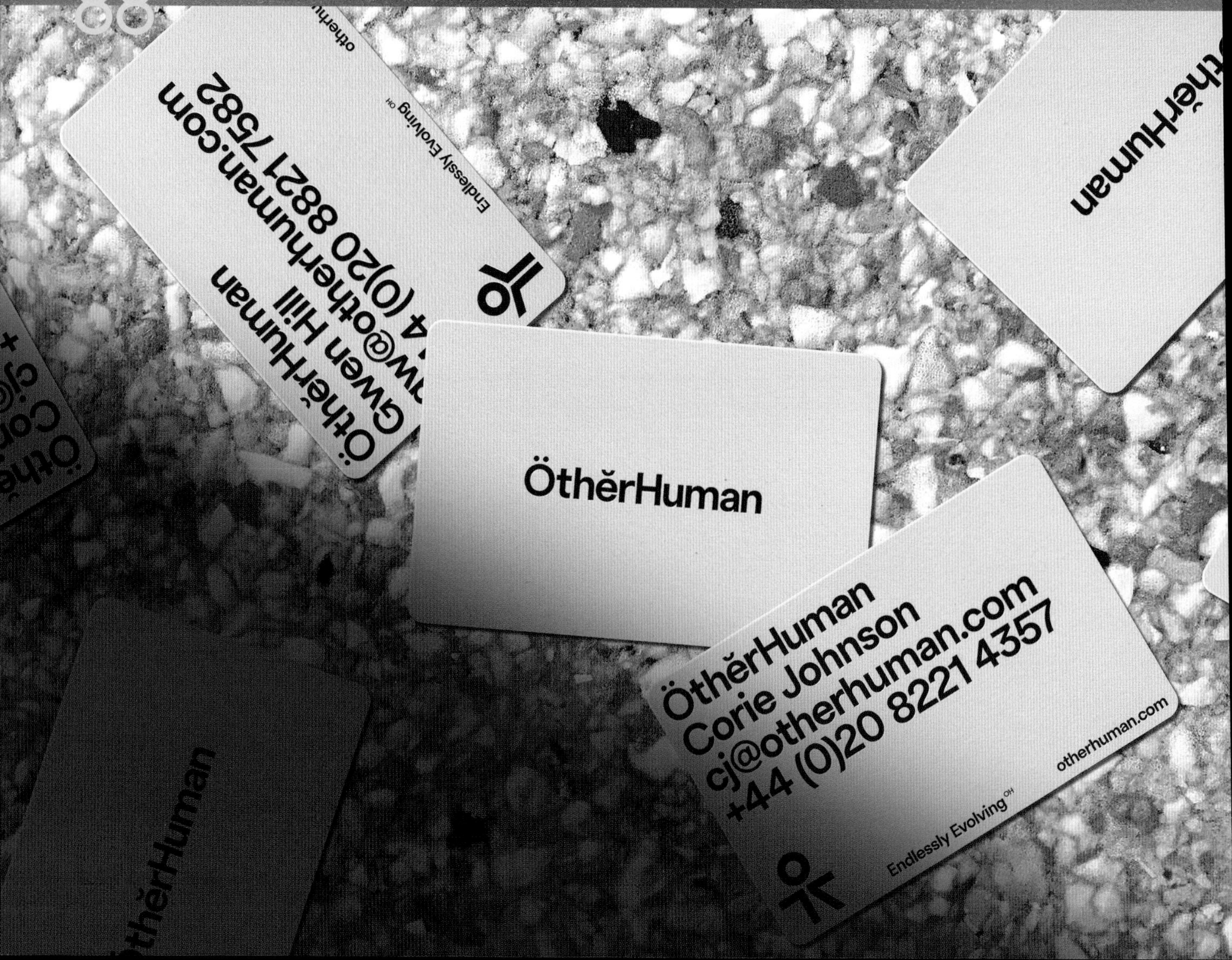

ŌthĕrHuman
Gwen Hill
gw@otherhuman.com
+44 (0)20 8821 7582

Endlĕssly Evölving ᴼᴴ

ŌthĕrHuman

ŌthĕrHuman

ŌthĕrHuman
Corie Johnson
cj@otherhuman.com
+44 (0)20 8221 4357

otherhuman.com

Endlĕssly Evölving ᴼᴴ

ŌthĕrHuman

THE GOAL WAS TO DISTIL VARIOUS HUMAN STANCES
AND POSITIONS DOWN TO THEIR SIMPLEST FORMS. ●

89

5AM START OR 5AM FINISH

FIRST CHOICE

⊗ RAGGED EDGE
→ raggededge.com

First Choice is the holiday company that lets you pick the trip you really want. Ragged Edge created a brand to propel this former British travel icon into the minds of a whole new generation, making First Choice the first choice for holidaymakers once again.

    The design system is built around a set of icons that represent the ability to curate the perfect combination of experiences for you. At the pool, up a mountain, in a city or by the sea. The choice is yours.

    They come together in an immediately distinctive logo that puts your choice first. And they live in every part of the experience. From functional signposting in the digital product, right through to expressive storytelling in comms. ●

HEYDAY

⊕ ORDER
→ order.design

Heyday is a productivity tool and browser extension that collects, connects, and organises all your research, automatically. Its adaptable system eliminates the tedious work previously required to stay organised and gives you the freedom to focus on your work.

On the heels of a new name and strategic positioning, Order built a versatile identity system that showcases the core functions of the product in an immediate, recognisable way. ●

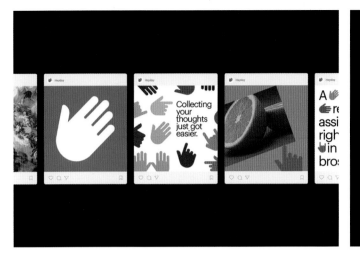

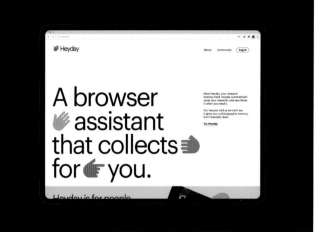

ORDER BUILT A VERSATILE IDENTITY SYSTEM THAT SHOWCASES THE CORE FUNCTIONS OF THE PRODUCT IN AN IMMEDIATE, RECOGNISABLE WAY. ●

day automatically saves
r research, and resurfaces
hen you need it.

started at heyday.xyz

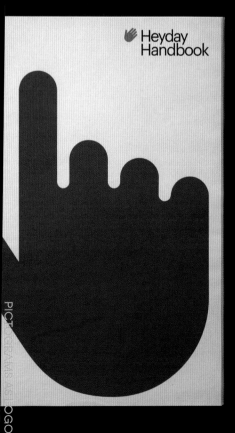

Heyday
Handbook

Team Manual 2021

Team Manual 2021

KINDERKLUBB

☘ MAX FRIEDMAN
→ maxbfriedman.com

Kinderklubb's mission is to improve the health and happiness of little kids by taking them on a journey of food discovery and adventure with fun and age-appropriate content. Think Anthony Bourdain for toddlers!

The identity centers around a simple geometric mark representing a smiley face, building blocks, and a bowl of food. It's accompanied by a custom wordmark that's equal parts clear (for parents) and playful (for kids). ●

THE IDENTITY CENTERS AROUND
A SIMPLE GEOMETRIC MARK
REPRESENTING A SMILEY FACE,
BUILDING BLOCKS, AND A BOWL
OF FOOD. ●

96

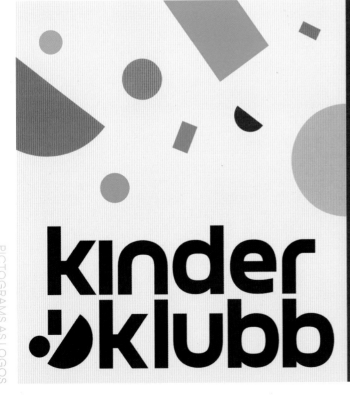

幸邻 All day Every
9.00-　23.00
day 岂止一次

幸邻
12.24
圣诞快乐 Xmas Special

幸
Sp
春

9.00-
23.00
岂止一次
幸邻 All day Every

幸邻

All day
Every
day

幸邻

All day
Every
day

幸邻
All day
Every
9.00 day
23.00
岂止一次

幸邻
All day
Every
9.00 day
23.00
岂止一次

幸邻 9.00-
23.00
All day Every
day 岂止一次

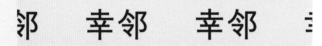

XING LIN 幸邻

⊟ MEAT
→ meat.studio

Xing Lin 幸邻 is a community building restaurant that remixes many cuisines into affordable meals.

The logo and visual identity is neutral, focusing on the economical use of visual grammar and syntax. The typography plays with the notion of proximity, reminiscent of a light and brief conversation between strangers at a restaurant. The layout system is loose yet orderly, intentionally mundane.

The iconography, typography, and colours are inspired by road signs, a classic and universal vernacular. The human figure, using the same stroke weight as the typeface, is a symbol of a friend, iconic but unintrusive. The identity treats the audience as a fellow human being, duly respected and warmly welcomed. ●

99

THE LOGO AND VISUAL IDENTITY IS NEUTRAL, FOCUSING ON THE ECONOMICAL USE OF VISUAL GRAMMAR AND SYNTAX. ●

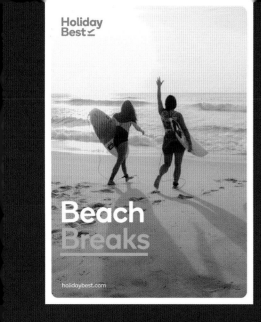

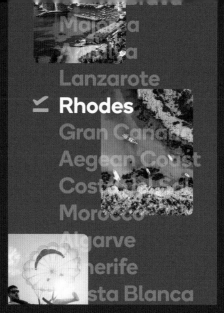

HOLIDAY BEST

✤ FELLOW
→ fellowstudio.com

A brand system was developed that utilised an 'underline' highlighting device to define what 'best' entails for Holiday Best, emphasising key benefits and experiences individuals seek in their holiday.

The underline motif also took the form of the aviation symbol within the primary logo lock-up. Drawing inspiration from the departures symbol familiar at airports, a symbol was crafted embodying the concept of 'Defining best'. Resembling not only a check-box but also a plane taking off to a sun-kissed destination. ●

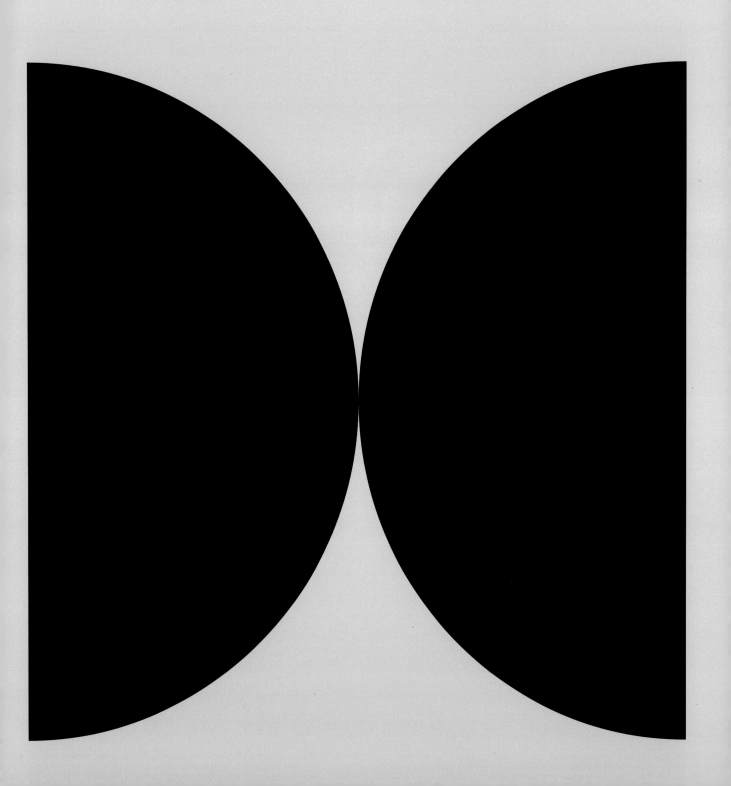

EPSOM VILLAGE

✤ DATE OF BIRTH
→ dateofbirth.com.au

Epsom Village is a colourful shopping community in Epsom, Victoria that has become the fastest growing retail centre in the fastest growing residential catchment of Bendigo, Victoria.

Date Of Birth were approached by NRG Property to create a rebrand to coincide with the revitalisation and redevelopment of the existing Epsom Village shopping complex, with the aim of making the development a hub for small business growth and a strong community. ●

HOAM MUSEUM
OF ART

🎨 ORDINARY PEOPLE
→ ordinarypeople.kr

The renewed identity for the Hoam Museum of Art symbolises a staircase that connects tradition and the future. Just like the stairs that go both upward and downward, as well as in two directions, the Hoam Museum of Art provides us with timeless values, preserving and passing on tradition and history while inspiring new thoughts about the future.

The identity is constructed proportionally based on the ratio of 4:3:2:1, inspiration from the staircase motif. These proportions signify tradition and history while also hinting at the progressive path toward the future. They are flexible and can be adapted as needed, such as 3:2:1 or 4:3, across various media and contexts.

Through the unified approach, from the logo to the signage, the entire museum is enveloped in a consistent form, establishing the unique visual identity of the Hoam Museum of Art. ●

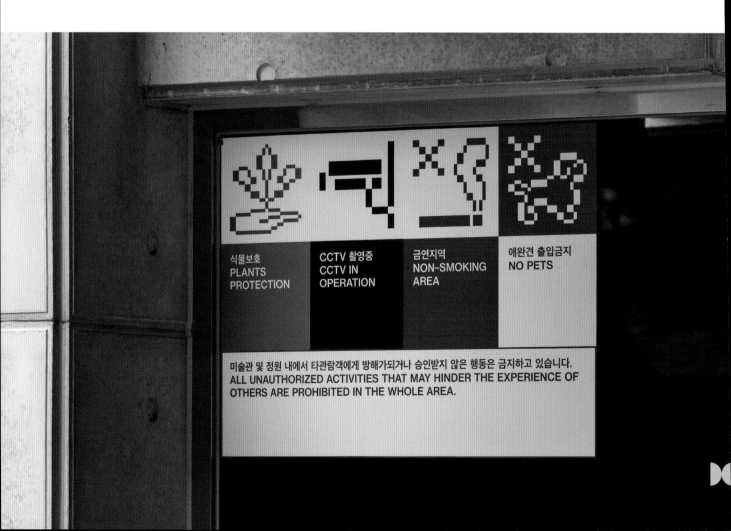

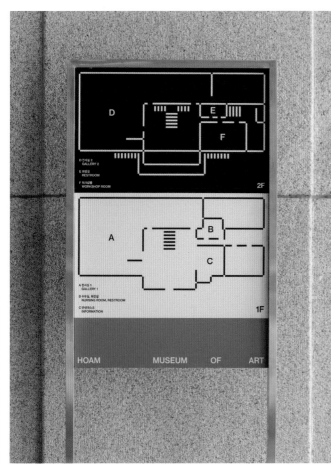

THROUGH THE UNIFIED APPROACH, FROM THE LOGO
TO THE SIGNAGE, THE ENTIRE MUSEUM IS ENVELOPED
IN A CONSISTENT FORM, ESTABLISHING THE UNIQUE
VISUAL IDENTITY OF THE HOAM MUSEUM OF ART. ●

HERE EAST

DNCO
→ dnco.com

London's home for making – Here East is a new campus in East London for businesses pushing technology and entrepreneurs creating smart and connected products. DNCO created a wayfinding system to navigate Here East's 1.2 million sq ft that is inspiring and intuitive to this specialist audience.

Directional arrows show the flow of energy. Reception desks are gateways to the next area, or transistors. Motors signify lifts. As in a circuit, the symbols are joined by lines to form a giant floor graphic connecting the whole campus.

DNCO CREATED A WAYFINDING SYSTEM TO NAVIGATE HERE EAST'S 1.2 MILLION SQ FT THAT IS INSPIRING AND INTUITIVE TO THIS SPECIALIST AUDIENCE.

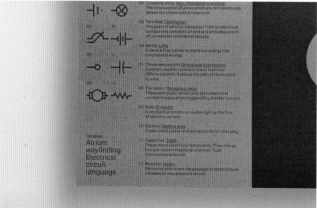

PATRICK ELEY & JOHN WYNNE

DNCO → DNCO.COM

 INTERVIEW

☻ THE SUCCESS OF A PICTOGRAM WILL DEPEND ON PEOPLE'S ABILITY TO DECODE IT. SOME GAIN RECOGNITION THROUGH REPETITION WHILE SOME ARE BETTER UNDERSTOOD, OR MIGHT BE TABOO, IN ONE CULTURE BUT NOT IN ANOTHER. ☻

⌨ Pictograms and icons often need to convey complex ideas in a simple visual form. How do you approach the challenge of simplification while maintaining clarity and meaning in your designs?

An idea older than hieroglyphics, icons are fascinating things. At their best they communicate effortlessly across language barriers with a clarity tempered by wit and elegance. At their worst they are illegible, confusing or misleading and sometimes even down-right dangerous.

The first questions we like to ask therefore, are about audience and context – who are the icons for, where will they be seen and what are people already familiar with. Icons are a short-hand so they will be far more successful if we design something that reflects existing experience and convention rather than starting from scratch every time. Will designing a pictogram for a spiral staircase, for example, really help us navigate when the basic stepped line neatly describes the experience of climbing any set of stairs, spiral or otherwise? As typographer Zuzana Licko once said, 'we read best what we read most'. However, icons replace words rather than sentences and while they need to be easily and quickly understood, some ideas or instructions are just too complex to be translated into an effective design. So it's important that we start with the simplest version of an idea in order to create the strongest icon. But while simplification can be critical for clarity, icons should not be overly simplistic. Reduction if taken to the extreme, can skirt dangerously close to illegibility.

Then there is the question of tone and character and where on the spectrum between abstract and representative the icons should sit. Are they solid or outlined, organic or geometric, stylised or illustrative? It's going to be more coherent if everything follows the same design principles. All the while we need to consider the wider brand and identity so that the icons we create feel a part of this language, whether that's following stylistic conventions such as reflecting the angles and forms of the typography, or more conceptual parameters such as the purpose and positioning behind the brand itself.

Icons are a code that needs to be learned. Sometimes people arrive already knowing the code, and sometimes they need to learn it as they go. In that case it's important to consider where the icons appear and whether there's anything we can add to help a user decode them. Icons should work without text[1], however making sure an icon sits alongside a written explanation can help embed the meaning and speed up the interpretation the next time it's seen.

[1] The ISO 7001 Guidelines suggest that to be accepted a pictogram has to be correctly interpreted by 80% of people with less than 10% of people interpreting the exact reverse meaning {what's known as the 80/10 rule}.

⌨ How does the design of pictograms and icons differ when creating for print versus digital platforms, and what considerations do you take into account for each medium?

Along with being clear and coherent, one of our key mantras is consistency – icon design shouldn't vary across different media. Reading from paper is a different experience than reading from a screen and arguments abound over which allows us to retain more information, but either way, print and digital need to align so there is no confusion in users' minds when switching between the two. That said, clarity at scale is critical. The magnification possible on screen means we are all able to see icons larger or smaller than they might ideally have been designed for. Screen resolution is getting so fine now that it's often in print where concessions have to be made. The maps we created for the V&A were the same online, in printed guides and on signs mounted on the walls of the galleries, but the icons we designed for the printed map differed subtly from the digital versions. We created ink traps in certain icons so that they didn't close up and enlarged some of the negative spaces – for example the arms and legs of the figures were moved further from the body so they remained clearly defined. The digital equivalent of this requires you to position icons cleanly on the pixel grid to avoid the shading and distortion that happens when they're out of alignment.

⌨ Icons and pictograms can be used for various purposes, from signage to user interfaces. What are some common challenges you face in adapting your designs to different applications, and how do you address them?

The biggest challenge is one of context – where icons appear affects both how they look, but also what they mean. On a computer screen, for example, the mouse pointer – an arrow pointing roughly north-north-west – indicates 'you are here', whereas if used in wayfinding it would more likely suggest 'you should go there'. Similarly, the X icon on a user interface usually means cancel an action or close an open window, but it means 'No Entry' when seen on signage. These are subtle differences, but understanding the environment in which an icon is seen helps us create an appropriate solution and one that will apply universally across different applications.

⌨ In your experience, how do cultural differences affect the interpretation of pictograms and icons? Can you provide examples of how you've adapted your designs for different cultural contexts?

The success of a pictogram will depend on people's ability to decode it. Some gain recognition through repetition while some are better understood, or might be taboo, in one culture but not in another – representations of the human body can be particularly contentious for example. As part of their research, the designers for the AIGA set of icons created in the 1980s used a way of assessing the strengths and weaknesses of the proposed pictograms which is still relevant today. They first looked at the semantic dimension; how well the symbol represents the message being depicted. They then considered the syntactic relationship; how the parts of the symbols relate to each other and whether the symbols form a consistent family. The final aspect was the pragmatic dimension; how well the pictogram performs, whether it be read at different sizes, affected by different lighting conditions or when viewed at different angles[2]. It's the semantic layer that we need to be particularly sensitive to, as cultural differences occur both within and across different populations – a teenager's frame of reference will be very different from a pensioner's.

...chronisms do occur, however. Children still understand the phone handset icon even though the objects themselves are increasingly obsolete, and the reel-to-reel icon is still used to indicate voicemail when cassette technology all but disappeared at the turn of the millennium. Icons like these endure through cultural inertia and collective memory which is always important to respect.

One question often asked by clients is how to sign a toilet, particularly in light of debates around gender and accessibility. If successful pictograms are visual representations of what you will find at your destination, then toilet signs often go against the flow, indicating who is allowed to use the space rather than what you'll actually find there. It's a subtle difference and one that is rarely questioned. Perhaps toilet taboo means we don't like talking about human waste or the mechanics of a system we're all intimately familiar with. On top of that, the stylised stick figures that stand in for different users can be seen as both anatomically and sartorially incorrect – they don't always make sense, nor are they particularly inclusive.

All-gender toilets have been standard in many places for a long time – on planes, trains, in our own homes – they're not a new idea, although in a society where gender identity is becoming ever more fluid they invoke a complex, charged debate. So how do we indicate what's behind the door in the simplest way possible? Combining male and female icons into a single figure is a frequent solution, but it feels reductionist and ultimately to be missing the point. People aren't half of one thing and half of another – they're complete individuals and hard to simplify. In a world where many people don't even identify as one gender or another, a merged set of symbols feels both redundant as well as unclear.

It turns out that the answer lies in going back to basics. Research has shown that the literal icon of a toilet, however squeamish this makes some feel, is the preferred option, which makes perfect sense given that we're happy with a coffee cup standing in for a cafe. There is a preference for the face-on view of a toilet rather than the side view and when words are also used, then the simpler and more generic WC or Restroom is the more inclusive choice.

²Symbol Signs: The system of passenger/pedestrian oriented symbols prepared by the American Institute of Graphic Arts, New York: Hastings House, 1981

Could you discuss your favourite project including pictograms or icons and the story behind it? What makes it stand out among your body of work?

Although icons are often meant to transcend words you do have to consider the different languages of your audience, not all of which are spoken. When designing many of the pictograms we created for the wayfinding at Here East we didn't follow the standard, familiar forms. Instead we thought about the type of people that would be using the spaces. Here East is a campus on the Olympic Park in London made for innovators and tech visionaries, so we created a set of icons that borrowed from the language of electronic circuitry familiar to this community. The atriums were hand-painted with bright orange icons at vast scales across walls and floors which brought energy and dynamism to these airport-scale spaces.

Some were tongue-in-cheek, others more literal – directional arrows marked the flow of people; reception desks, the gateways to a visitor's onward journey, were transistors; motors signified lifts and batteries represented seating as places to rest and recharge. As in a circuit, the symbols were joined by lines to form a super-graphic connecting the whole campus. It's a memorable design, perhaps a little gratuitous in parts, but like any good wayfinding positively adds to the sense of place.

For aspiring designers looking to integrate pictogram and icon design into their work, what advice would you give them? Are there key skills or practices they should prioritise in their journey?

Designing icons isn't usually a quick process; simplification takes time. Practice reducing things to their most basic forms, but think about what is the most defining characteristic that needs to remain for the form to be recognisable. Icon design shares a lot with caricature in that you need to exaggerate unique features so that they can be easily distinguished. Water coming from a shower head for example looks nothing like its depiction in an icon – droplets that size would be as big as tennis balls. Similarly, scale across different icons in a set is quite a fluid concept – you might use a cup to indicate a cafe, which when drawn as an icon appears the same size as a car. Thankfully, we tend to ignore these fluctuations, as long as icons all share the same stylistic principles.

Sometimes the slightest change in the angle of a line can convey dramatically different meanings. Humans are very attuned to faces and body shapes and able to project meaning and emotion into the simplest of representations – the huge variety of emojis just goes to show how nuanced you can be with very few components. A circle with two dots will be read as a face whether we like it or not, so don't ignore your subjective gut-feeling to a form as well looking at it from an objective point of view.

Before starting the design process make sure that the list of icons is clearly defined so you can be sure the principles you set will work across everything without having to be adjusted later. Start with some basic icons first and then build out from those – those showing people can often give a particular character or energy to the set so are a good starting point to explore different styles. Once you have decided on what works for the simple icons you can apply the successful design elements to the more complex ones.

Everything needs to occupy the same volume and also fit within a consistently-sized canvas.

It's also important to consider the hierarchy of how the icons will sit together on an application – there's little point in designing the lift and stair icon separately only to discover that they clash horribly when placed side-by-side on a sign.

It's usually a good idea to keep the perspective the same – don't mix 2D and 3D elements, and try to use similar viewing angles so that icons are either all seen from the same position, or a limited number of views. However, if something is more recognisable from one angle then think carefully about going against expectations; a bicycle doesn't look much like a bicycle when viewed from above. It's never a good idea to forgo legibility at the expense of a rigid system.

Generally speaking, icons either depict objects or actions. Objects are often simpler to define as there is something physical to stylise, but actions can be trickier as there are many ways to represent the same result. So keep an open mind. The most important thing is to put yourself in someone else's position – never assume that your references are universal and that people will see the same way that you do. ●

SCHRODERS

⌗ DNCO
→ dnco.com

Schroders' move to London Wall Place, an imposing new building by Make Architects, marked the coming together of their many London offices under one roof for the first time. This meant more than a new home, but a new way of working.

Schroders divided their space in two – the upper floors for quiet meetings with private clients and the lower floors for team collaboration. The challenge was to create a unified wayfinding language which could vary in tone, but stay consistent across these different environments.

The client-facing floors required a discreet hotel-level treatment, in keeping with tp Bennett's interiors. DNCO specified anodised, waterjet-cut, aluminium letters with hidden fixings to complement the elegant material palette and introduced a refined hanging line to anchor and frame the elements on the various surfaces throughout the space.

The line language was extended into a bolder expression on the team floors with tactile square-fluted panels acting as a container to hold wayfinding information. They cut into the fluting at vertical circulation points with supergraphic floor numbers and glazed, simply updatable sign panels. Projecting signs displayed their bespoke icon set, developed to complement the sans serif typography used throughout the system – DNCO believe even toilet signs deserve to be beautiful. ●

SOLO SAUNA TUNE

⌂ STUDY LLC. / TAKAHIRO ETO
→ studyllc.tokyo

This identity and signage design was created for a sauna, which offers an authentic Finnish-style experience in a completely private room. Considering that it is the first solo sauna in Japan and located in Kagurazaka, the designer combines the four letters of 'tune' in the brand name into a square shape to create a crest for the logo. This graphic is applied to curtains, paper lanterns and uniforms to form a visual identity with an English name but a Japanese look. STUDY LLC. also used common elements within the signs, icons, and numbers to create a consistent visual thread throughout the details. ●

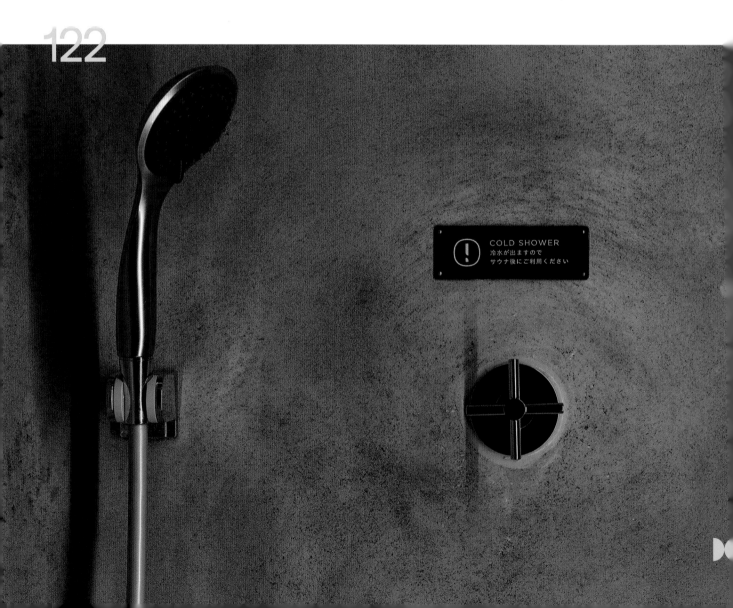

How to use
Solo Sauna tune
ソロサウナtuneの利用方法

 SHOWER
洗体

∨

 SAUNA
サウナ

∨

 COLD
SHOWER
冷水浴

∨

 REST
休憩

∨

 CHECKOUT
会計

×2,3

ROOM

2

ROOM

3

ROOM

4

SHISEIDO BEAUTY SITE SIGN SYSTEM

STUDY LLC. / TAKAHIRO ETO
→ studyllc.tokyo

Shiseido BEAUTY SITE is a tour facility of Shiseido Osaka Ibaraki Factory. The concept is 'The Journey to Beauty'. Visitors can enjoy learning about manufacturing while touring various areas such as the museum, lab, and marché. Signs resembling traffic signs, bus stops, and house number signs are scattered throughout the facility to create a town-like atmosphere. The high saturation colours of the signs reflect on the white walls, giving the white-based space a subtlety and elegance. These signs stand out as key elements of the interior, making the factory tour experience a journey. ●

Creative Direction:
Tetsuro Kanegae / Shiseido Company, Limited,
Rikiya Uekusa / Shiseido Company, Limited

Art Direction:
Takahiro Eto / STUDY LLC, Rena Uemura,
Shiseido Creative Co., Ltd.

Takumi Ota / Takumi Ota Photography Co., Ltd.

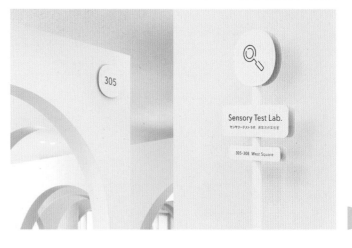

Materials House

マテリアルハウス 原材料庫

303, 304 South Street

Point
2

原料保管
Raw material storage
原料保管

温度・湿度

温度が高くなったり、空気中の水分を含む

性質が変わってしまう原料があります。

品質を保つために最適な温湿度条件で保

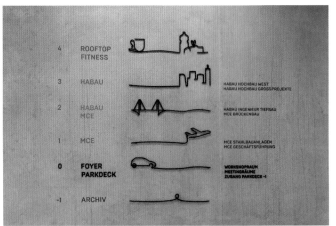

HAB25

🎴 MOOI DESIGN
→ mooi-design.com

HAB25 was constructed as the new headquarter of HABAU GROUP – an international, full-service provider for all areas of construction – under the principles of the New Work paradigm. MOOI DESIGN translated their corporate design into corporate architecture. As a result, a wholesome approach of light, colour, form, and tangible values originated. The highly flexible work environment is reflected in the workspace design and the signage concept. Custom-illustrated icons and handwritten typography serve as a guidance system.

The playful single-line forms and unique production from construction site materials create a strong, recognisable brand and enhance the user experience at the same time. ●

THE PLAYFUL SINGLE-
LINE FORMS AND UNIQUE
PRODUCTION FROM
CONSTRUCTION SITE
MATERIALS CREATE A
STRONG, RECOGNISABLE
BRAND AND ENHANCE
THE USER EXPERIENCE
AT THE SAME TIME. ●

131

QUEENSTOWN AIRPORT

⊕ MAKEBARDO
→ makebardo.com

MAKEBARDO's team was hired to redesign the wayfinding system for Queenstown Airport in New Zealand. The airport aims to provide an efficient and top-notch facility that reflects the best of the region. MAKEBARDO worked closely with the airport team to understand their needs and prioritised a customer-centred approach throughout the creative process. They referred to the airport's affordable, adaptable, sustainable, and memorable principles to guide their work.

MAKEBARDO created a unique, functional, and recognisable signage system that appeals to multiple audiences, emphasising the concept of 'Making the invisible visible'. The system visualises the invisible lines created when people travel from one place to another, using a flexible, modular, and scalable identity of three intuitive and friendly lines. They also designed a bespoke set of pictograms, which they super-sized to enhance the visitor experience. ●

◉ Michael Thomas

V&A

DNCO
→ dnco.com

Over the last ten years, visitor numbers at the V&A have tripled. In order to protect its future, DNCO were asked to create a comprehensive wayfinding system to enable the V&A's four million annual visitors to explore the museum with confidence and curiosity.

One of the most significant innovations in this system is the use of colour. Reserving it as a highlight purely for paid exhibitions, colour acts as a beacon drawing visitors through the busy ground floor and getting them to their destinations faster – thus protecting a core revenue stream that helps keep the permanent galleries free to explore. The colour is specific to each exhibition and is consistently used from tube ad to entry signage. ●

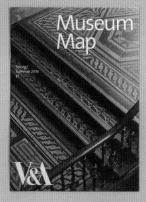

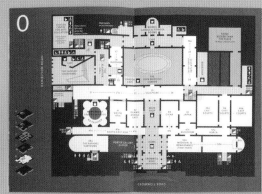

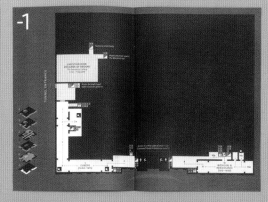

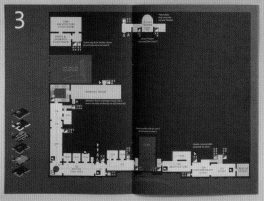

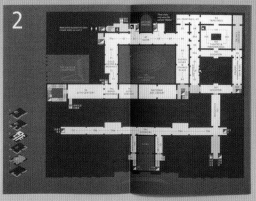

LEEUM MUSEUM OF ART

⚇ ORDINARY PEOPLE
→ ordinarypeople.kr

Ordinary People's task was to build a design system, stemming from the new logo, to be applied to the museum's various communication channels, such as stationery, signage, website, membership publications, etc. They focused on creating a versatile graphic system, applicable and adaptable across all kinds of media, while maintaining consistency in the visual identity of the new logo, as well as the overall look of the renovation project. ●

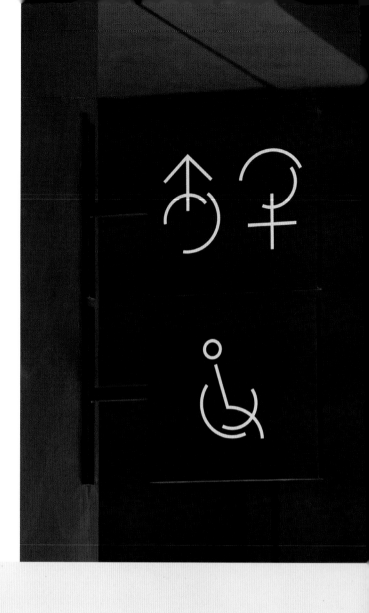

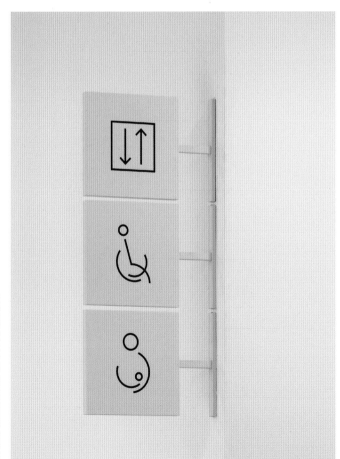

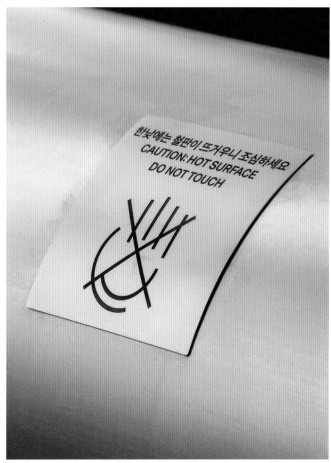

중력의 역방향	Ephemeral Gravity	→
1		
이상한 행성	Strange Planet	↙
B1		

140

루이즈 부르주아
숲(밤의 정원)

Louise Bourgeois
Forest (Night Garden)

1953
청동에 갈색과 검정색 파티나, 흰색 페인트

1953
Bronze with brown, black patina, white paint

눈으로만 봐주세요
DO NOT TOUCH

손끼임 주의
DOOR CLOSES AUTOMATICALLY
WATCH YOUR HANDS

손대지 마세요
DO NOT TOUCH

기대지 마세요
DO NOT LEAN AGAINST DOOR

손끼임 주의
DOOR CLOSES AUTOMATICALLY
WATCH YOUR HANDS

In-image text: Ready, set, go! Hit the green button and see how quickly you can run up the 106 steps

EDINBURGH PARK

⊗ DNCO
→ dnco.com

1 New Park Square at Edinburgh Park is a bold response from architects AHMM to sweeping views of the Pentland Hills. DNCO's elegant, yet opinionated, wayfinding underlines the rich textures of this new place.

A beautiful interplay between materials arises as the cut edges of the dark green signs are painted in a brighter, contrasting green.

DNCO designed a bespoke icon set as part of the building identity with a powerful, simple geometry, also based on the angular serifs of the Beirut typeface. ●

of
shifting
light
of
changing
skies

Bike store
Showers
Toilets

Accessible shower

Inspirational views over
the Pentland Hills

4

84,000 sq ft of lively
and flexible space

3

A community powered
by renewable energy

2

Inspirational workspace
designed for wellness

1

Patina bar/restaurant/bakery
Auditorium
Café

G

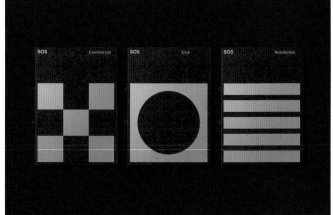

505

 SEACHANGE
→ seachange.studio

'505', a multifaceted construction company, sought a brand overhaul to distinguish themselves within commercial, civil, and residential sectors. Their name lacked memorability and relevance, so a mnemonic approach was adopted.

A symbolic logo, combining abstract '5', '0', and '5' numerals, embodies their three-pronged services: commercial (stacked squares), civil (abstract '0'), and residential (stacked bars). The versatile logo can adapt to various applications and environments.

A colour palette of ultramarine blue and concrete grey enhances visibility. The sleek, brutalist design caters to both rugged construction equipment and premium residential branding, ensuring instant recognition in the local construction industry. ●

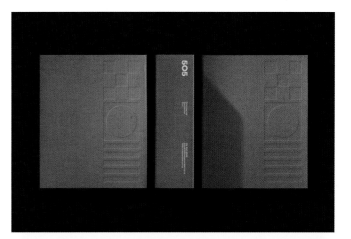

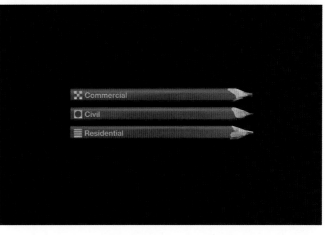

505

Commercial
Residential
Civil

09 392 950
info@505cc
505constru

MAS

 PAZ MIAMOR
→ pazmiamor.com

'MAS' is a human resources consulting firm based in Santiago, Chile. The new icon represents a multiplication, rather than an obvious addition, enhancing its concept and meaning.

The new graphic system provides easy identification of each business unit, while maintaining the versatility and autonomy of the main group identity. A limited colour palette is paired with grey backgrounds and a playful use of scale is utilised. The identity is clean and loud, simple and messy, serious and playful. ●

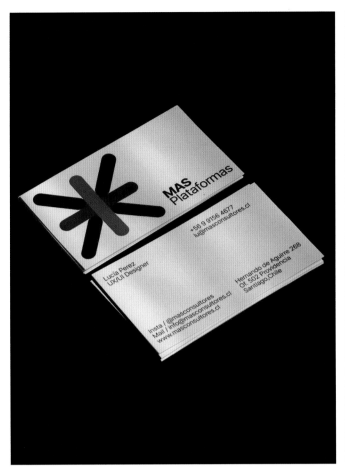

THE IDENTITY IS CLEAN AND LOUD, SIMPLE
AND MESSY, SERIOUS AND PLAYFUL. ●

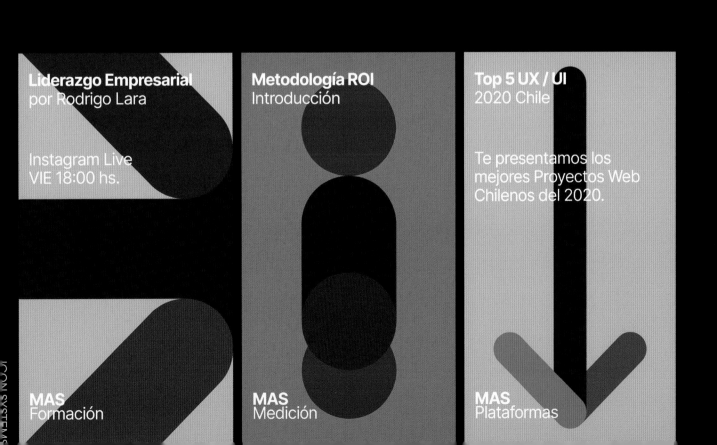

Liderazgo Empresarial
por Rodrigo Lara

Instagram Live
VIE 18:00 hs.

MAS
Formación

Metodología ROI
Introducción

MAS
Medición

Top 5 UX / UI
2020 Chile

Te presentamos los
mejores Proyectos Web
Chilenos del 2020.

MAS
Plataformas

MAS

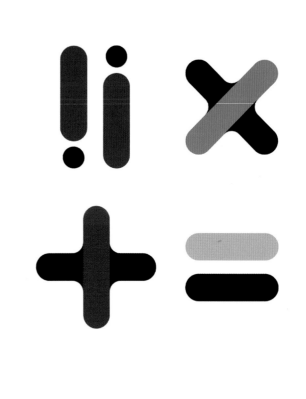

MAS
Grupo

MAS
Consultoría

MAS
Formación

MAS
Plataformas

MAS
Medición

MAS

MAS
Formación

MAS
Consultoría

JOHN
MASTRO

JOHN MASTRO → dateofbirth.com.au

INTERVIEW

⌨ Pictograms and icons often need to convey complex ideas in a simple visual form. How do you approach the challenge of simplification while maintaining clarity and meaning in your designs?

At Date Of Birth, tackling the challenge of simplifying pictograms and icons is like finding the perfect recipe – it's all about balance! We dive into the nitty-gritty, stripping away the non-essentials and distilling complex ideas into visually understandable forms. We're big on feedback and testing, making sure our designs hit that sweet spot between simplicity and clear communication.

⌨ How does the design of pictograms and icons differ when creating for print versus digital platforms, and what considerations do you take into account for each medium?

For print, we think about size, colors, and textures, ensuring our icons shine in every print format. On the digital runway, we're all about dynamic elements – animations, responsiveness – making sure our icons dance seamlessly with the overall user interface. It's like a well-choreographed performance in pixels!

⌨ In your experience, how do cultural differences affect the interpretation of pictograms and icons? Can you provide examples of how you've adapted your designs for different cultural contexts?

Icons speak a global language, but we know there are local dialects. We dig into the cultures, savoring the unique visual languages and nuances. Whether it's adjusting colors or adding a dash of local flair, we make sure our designs not only speak but sing in harmony with diverse audiences.

⌨ Could you discuss your favourite project including pictograms or icons and the story behind it? What makes it stand out among your body of work?

One of our most pertinent case studies revolves around a recent collaboration with an international travel retail brand. Our task was to develop an icon and logo system that not only ensured overall brand consistency but also uniquely resonated with the diverse cultures of each city. Despite the challenges, our guiding light throughout the project was the extensive research we conducted in tandem with the client and local consultants. It resulted in a neutral color scheme harmonizing seamlessly across cities, complemented by bespoke, simple icons. These icons artfully represented the distinctive landscapes of each city, serving as powerful identifiers for individual retail stores.

⌨ Icons and pictograms can be used for various purposes, from signage to user interfaces. What are some common challenges you face in adapting your designs to different applications, and how do you address them?

From signage to user interfaces, each platform has its unique requirements and nuances. Challenges naturally arise, encompassing factors like scalability, legibility, and context. However, we navigate these challenges by conducting thorough usability testing sessions. These sessions serve as a valuable forum for collecting feedback and refining our designs to ensure their effectiveness across diverse applications.

⌨ For aspiring designers looking to integrate pictogram and icon design into their work, what advice would you give them? Are there key skills or practices they should prioritise in their journey?

Approach your work with curiosity and simplicity. Embrace feedback as a valuable tool in your design process. Cultivate cultural awareness, exploring diverse visual languages. Hone your design skills meticulously, staying updated on industry trends. Collaborate effectively with diverse teams to enrich your perspective. Your journey into pictogram and icon design is not just a path, it's a professional adventure unfolding. ●

☻ APPROACH YOUR WORK WITH CURIOSITY AND SIMPLICITY. EMBRACE FEEDBACK AS A VALUABLE TOOL IN YOUR DESIGN PROCESS. CULTIVATE CULTURAL AWARENESS, EXPLORING DIVERSE VISUAL LANGUAGES. HONE YOUR DESIGN SKILLS METICULOUSLY, STAYING UPDATED ON INDUSTRY TRENDS. COLLABORATE EFFECTIVELY WITH DIVERSE TEAMS TO ENRICH YOUR PERSPECTIVE. ☻

THE GOAL WAS TO CREATE A UNIFORM IDENTITY THAT
COULD APPLY ACROSS THE COUNTRY BUT DISTINCTLY
IDENTIFY EACH CITY LOCATION. ●

ARI CANADA

❀ DATE OF BIRTH
→ dateofbirth.com.au

ARI is a global travel retailer with many duty free stores across multiple continents. Date Of Birth were tasked with rebranding their Canadian stores. The goal was to create a uniform identity that could apply across the country but distinctly identify each city location.

Date Of Birth created a contemporary design that drew inspiration from the past. Each icon created subtly told a story about the place making it easy to identify each city. To ensure this was communicated coherently they engaged with locals and travellers to ask what's distinctive about the city they're in or visiting. ●

THE IDENTITY TRIES TO REPRESENT THE DIFFERENT AREAS
OF THE BRAND THROUGH PORTALS THAT OPEN TO A NEW
WORLD OF ENERGY AND INFORMATION THAT CAN HELP
PEOPLE AND COMPANIES TO BE BETTER. ● CBA BUE ⋇

holistic
management

h⋇listic
management

HOL MANAGEMENT

⊕ PAZ MIAMOR
→ pazmiamor.com

Hol Management is a company that provides wellness tools to companies and individuals based on astrology and other holistic techniques such as meditation, mindfulness, yoga, and more.

The identity tries to represent the different areas of the brand through portals that open to a new world of energy and information that can help people and companies to be better.

Each icon is a portal that seems static but represents a movement, helping to display a dynamic system that prepares this brand for any possible scenario. ●

159

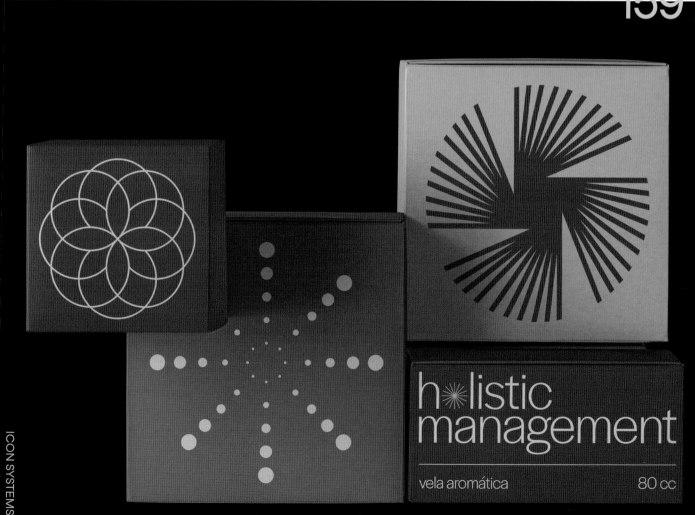

holistic
management

vela aromática   80 cc

holistic
management

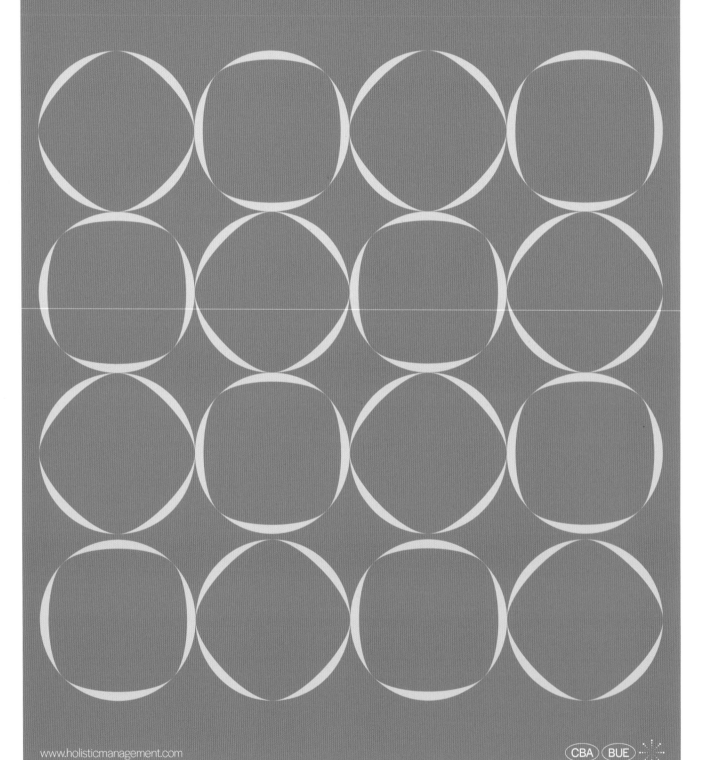

www.holisticmanagement.com

h✺listic
management

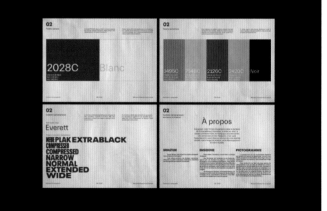

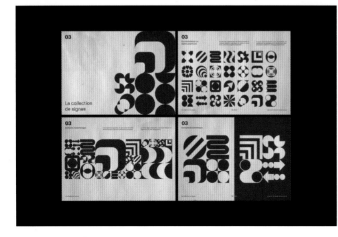

EXPOGRAPH

⊗ BRAND BROTHERS
→ brandbrothers.studio

Expograph is one of the major players in signage in France. Established in 1973 at the gateway to Paris, the group specialises in the design and manufacture of signage systems, visual communication and decoration. Signs, 3D letters, marking of buildings and offices; the company, which designs and manufactures all its products in-house, now boasts a high level of expertise. In the spring of 2019, Brand Brothers were asked to completely rethink the visual identity. The mantra: inform, guide, beautify.

Brand Brothers then, together with the communication team, refocused the approach towards a more radical, direct and raw axis, expressing technicality and systemic thinking through their graphic identity. The new logo, based on a custom typographic design, is a monochromatic typogram, whose characters have been designed on the basis of a series of identical rectangles.

The 'X', pointing in four directions, becomes the starting point of the new visual system: a collection of forms, which Brand Brothers constantly enrich, joining together infinitly and subtly to evoke the three great promises of the company. ●

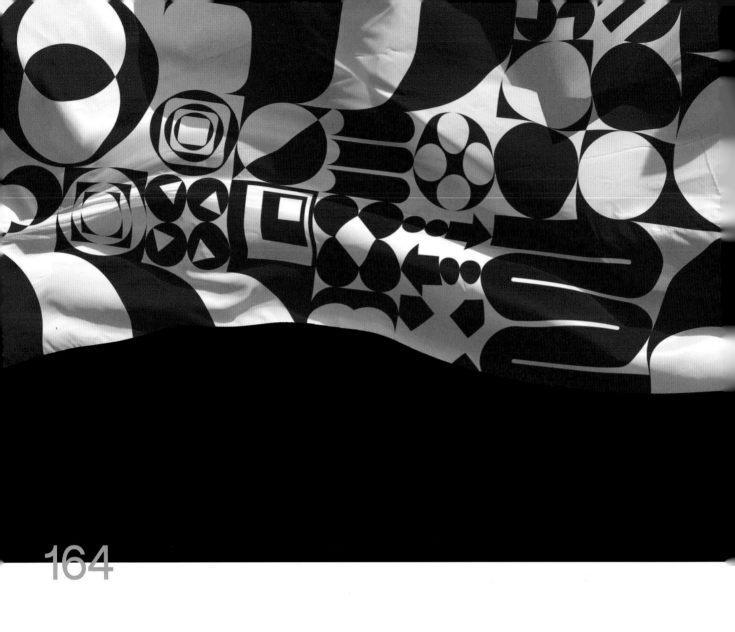

164

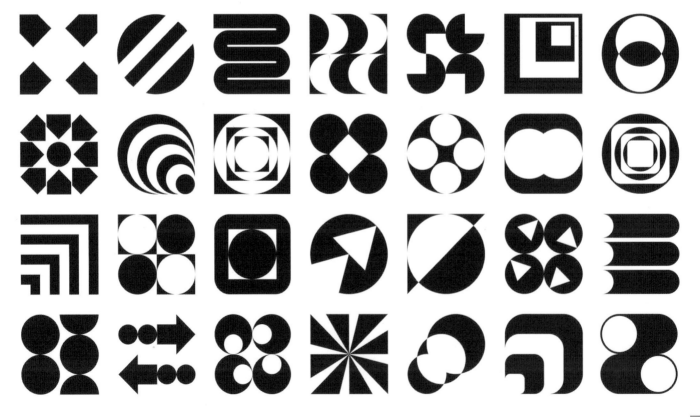

ICON SYSTEMS

INSTITUTE FOR INTERNATIONAL STUDIES

⌂ MADE
→ made-studio.ru

The Institute for International Studies is a recently established MGIMO University entity that provides expert reports for main government agencies engaged in formulating Russian foreign policy.

MADE created a logotype and identity for the institute. They built on the idea of reports as the client's main product and created a logo with simple elements that resemble books on a shelf. These elements serve as the identity's foundation. MADE created a series of icons for the various reports that have different meanings, but used just one element. This simple and practical approach allowed for a modern, and at the same time, diversified identity. ●

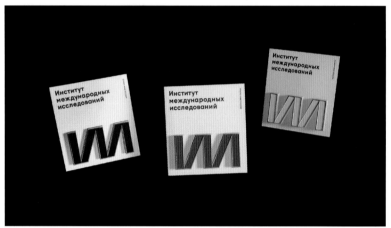

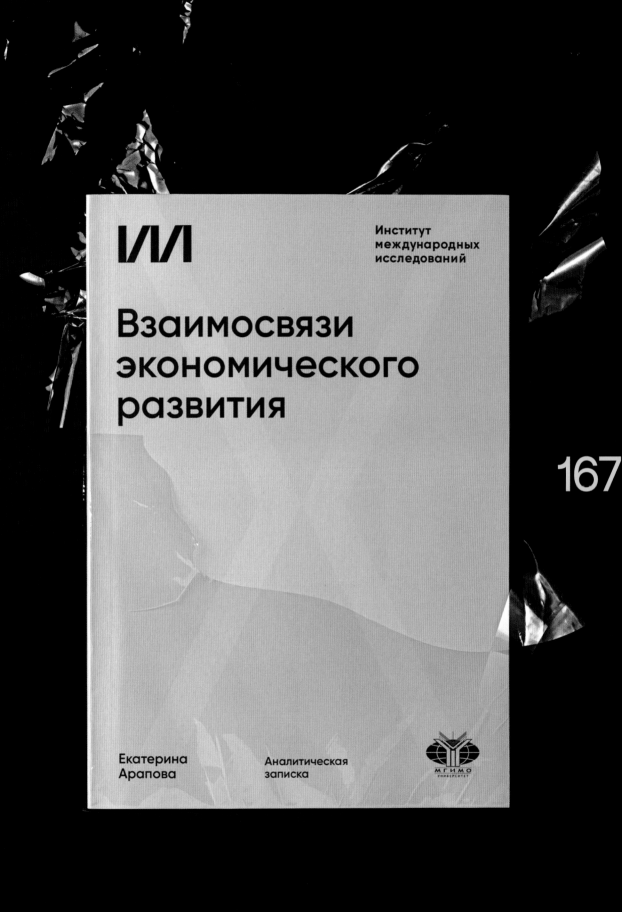

МГИМО Университет

Институт международных исследований

Взаимосвязи экономического развития

Екатерина Арапова

Аналитическая записка

167

MADE CREATED A SERIES OF ICONS FOR THE VARIOUS
REPORTS THAT HAVE DIFFERENT MEANINGS, BUT USED
JUST ONE ELEMENT. ●

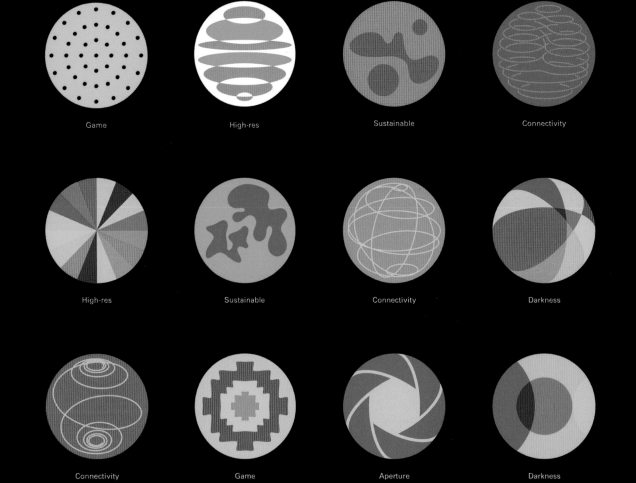

Game

High-res

Sustainable

Connectivity

High-res

Sustainable

Connectivity

Darkness

Connectivity

Game

Aperture

Darkness

SAMSUNG GALAXY S23

△ Studio Werk / Jaehoon Choi
→ werkgraphic.com

This project was created for the launch event of the Samsung Galaxy S23. Studio Werk focused on constructing a graphic identity that metaphorises the product's camera design without directly revealing the product, in order to create a fresh take on the event.

Using the camera design of the product ː three consecutive circles ː as a motif, Studio Werk organised graphic variations that convey the five points of the Galaxy S23: connectivity, high-res, sustainability, gaming, and darkness. The graphic images were installed on the exterior walls of a major downtown area in Seoul, changing the city's landscape for a short period of time. ●

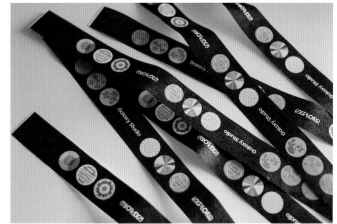

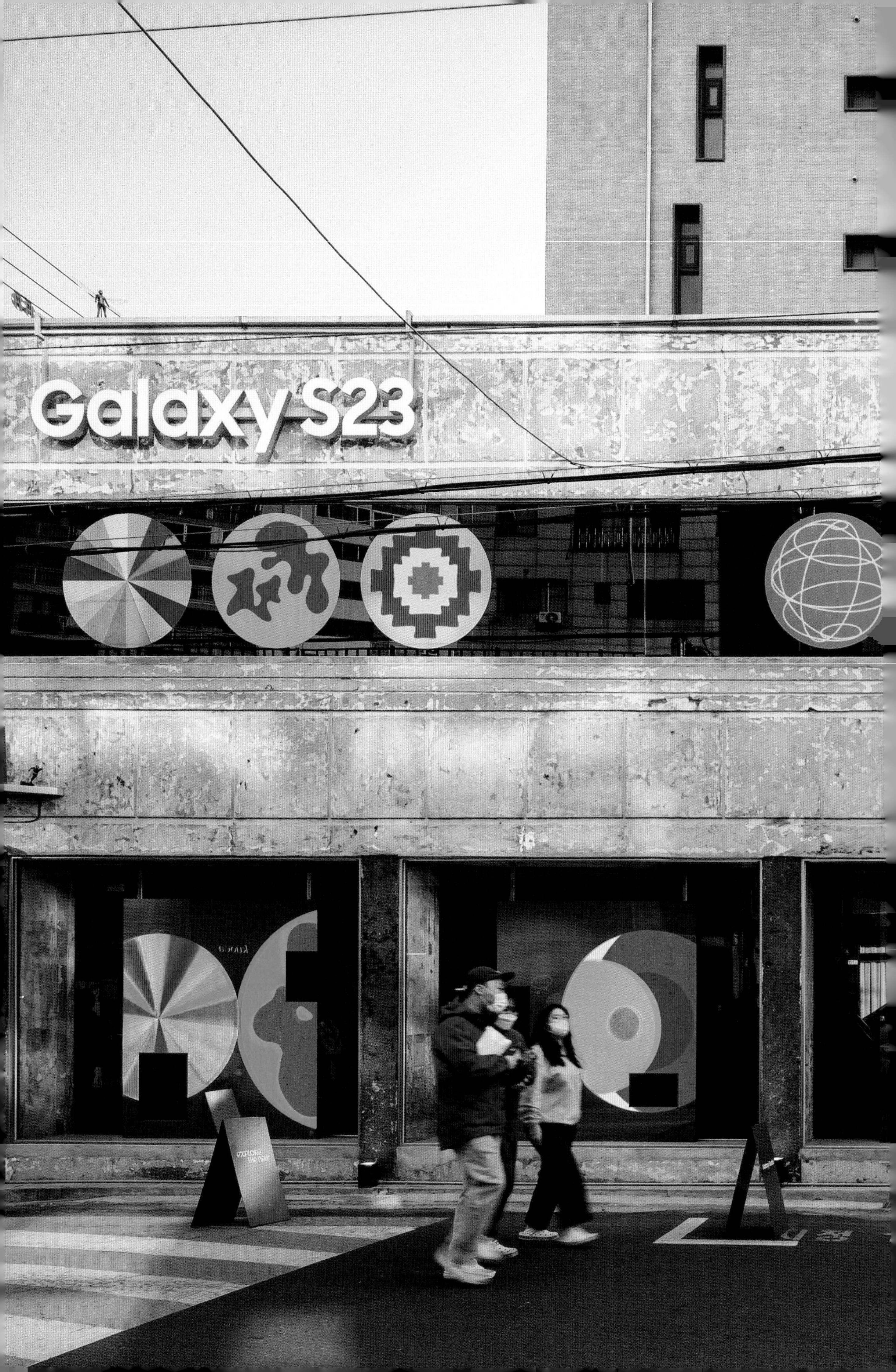
Galaxy S23

MYTHICAL STATE

⌂ SASYK MIHAL
→ sasyk.com

Mythical State is a brand selling merchandise, experiences, concepts and content. Mythical State is about transformation and transcendence as a result of outdoor sports and experiences, about 'Altered States & Rapture Moments'. Mythical State is the modern Vision Quest, an Endurance Cult.

They are not kitsch, ironic, or insincere. They genuinely believe in the power and utility of transformation and that experiences, especially difficult experiences, can and do serve as a portal or 'transformation' device. Outdoor experiences transform your geographic, mental, spiritual and physical 'particulars'. Pain and suffering, exposure to the elements, hunger, lack of sleep, shared experiences are a gateway to change.

For a very atypical brand Sasyk Mihal created an atypical brand system, using a huge assets library (containing a glyph set, shapes, custom typeface, motion, etc.) combined with bold colour and unique lay-outs. ●

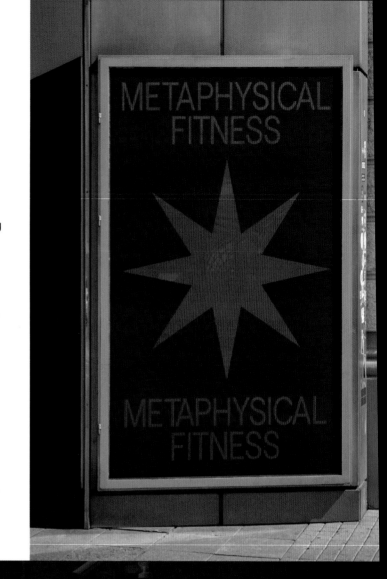

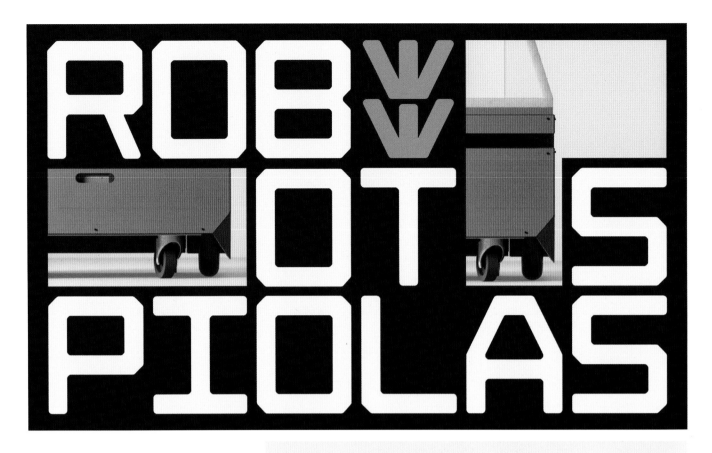

APELIE

⚅ PAZ MIAMOR
→ pazmiamor.com

'Let's make robots fun again, like when we were kids'.

Apelie is a new company that builds robots that help solve multi-area problems, from tiny to big ones.

The identity was inspired by car brands, which put an icon in front of the vehicle and the name behind it. A whole typography was developed for this, using the same main shapes for the icon and the logo.

The identity navigates between old and new feelings, binary language and symbols, inspired by the nostalgic emotions generated by brands like NASA, Nintendo and Star Wars. ●

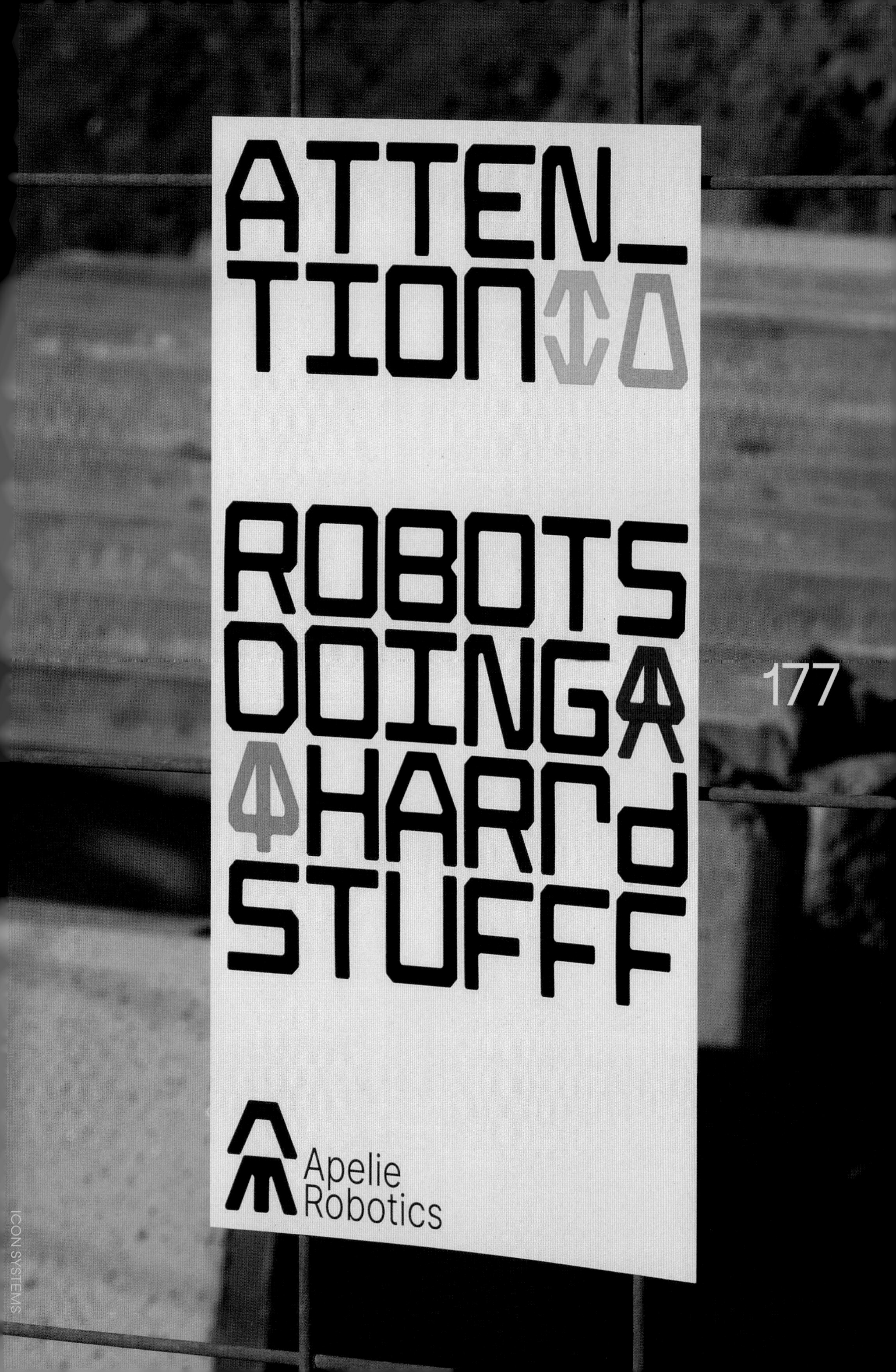

ATTEN_
TION TO

ROBOTS
DOING A
4 HARD
STUFFF

Apelie
Robotics

SHORT WAVES FESTIVAL 2021

UNIFORMA
→ uniforma.pl

Studio Uniforma has developed a flexible, year-round, partially animated visual identification system for the Short Waves Festival.

They took the risk of choosing uncompromising black and white and a seemingly clunky, 'newspaper-like' way of composing the design work, which stands out in the area of film events promotion.

The visual identity of the 2021 edition was based on the edition's slogan: Mirror Mirror. The mirror not only reflects reality, but creates it, which shows the complexity of living in the present.

The main theme of the entire visual identity – a mirror image in a box – reflects us, as people. In one reflection – it seems like a frame from the film, but the other remains unreadable: a reflection of reality, the ambiguity of the image, a deep journey into our psyche and much more, because everyone perceives the same reality in a different and unique way. ●

THE MAIN THEME OF THE
ENTIRE VISUAL IDENTITY –
A MIRROR IMAGE IN A BOX –
REFLECTS US, AS PEOPLE. ●

SHORT WAVES FESTIVAL

2021

13.

swf2021
mirrormirror

#

MIRROR
MIRROR

13.

14

ONLINE
STAY HOME
ONLINE ONLINE

OM73

events

7

International
Short Film
Festival

(2021)

13.

days

Poznań
& online

20.06

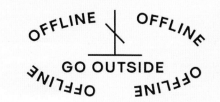
OFFLINE OFFLINE
GO OUTSIDE
OFFLINE OFFLINE

S
W
F
13.
2021

MICHELE
VERZE

MICHELE VERZE → micheleverze.com

INTERVIEW

to convey complex ideas in a simple visual form. How do you approach the challenge of simplification while maintaining clarity and meaning in your designs?

Metaphors serve as convenient shortcuts to convey complex concepts in a simplified manner, and icons and pictograms essentially represent straightforward visual metaphors. Throughout my creative process, I embrace a free-thinking, open-minded approach and amass information about my target audience. This profound understanding enables me to make informed decisions regarding the design, such as selecting the most appropriate metaphor, style, and level of detail. This ensures that my audience comprehends the message while maintaining a delicate balance between aesthetics and functionality. The aesthetic or design can manifest in various forms and can be as creative as desired. However, in my perspective, it should never compromise the core meaning and purpose of the icon or pictogram itself.

How does the design of pictograms and icons differ when creating for print versus digital platforms, and what considerations do you take into account for each medium?

The user experience varies significantly between print and digital mediums. While print presents certain technical limitations, the digital realm provides a broader array of possibilities. When working with print, I carefully consider factors like dimensions and paper stock to ensure optimal legibility, even at smaller sizes. However, digital allows me to think outside the box, enabling me to envision how the design will be displayed and interacted with, which opens a world of opportunities. In the digital landscape, icons can be visible for a long or a limited time, leading to considerations like colour changes, animations, and effects, among others.

In your experience, how do cultural differences affect the interpretation of pictograms and icons? Can you provide examples of how you've adapted your designs for different cultural contexts?

in my creative process, I have a strong desire to gain a deep understanding of my audience, to walk in their shoes, grasp their subtleties, and comprehend their interactions with the world. Factors such as language, cultural background, religion, and educational levels, among others, force me to tailor my approach and design accordingly. A few years ago, I worked on an award-winning project called 'Rescue Rashie', which involved designing a swimming rash vest for children with CPR instructions cleverly printed on it. One of my primary challenges was finding a solution to display crucial step-by-step instructions and establish a style for pictograms that would be as clear as possible for parents or bystanders who might experience fear or panic while attempting to rescue a child.

For a digital start-up named Formm, I created a set of icons tailored to the Formm industry and its clients. The concept for these icons materialised as I immersed myself over a multitude of pitch decks, PowerPoint slides, reports, and various documents from both our internal archives and those of competitors and the wider web. Once I identified a common thread, the execution resulted in a visual language that was simple yet dynamic, in line with the agility that characterises a start-up.

Could you discuss your favourite project including pictograms or icons and the story behind it? What makes it stand out among your body of work?

While working on the revamp of print collaterals for a renowned tax services company, we came to a significant realisation: taxes are often overwhelming for most people, and they don't typically find the topic inspiring. Our task was to create a fresh look and feel that could instil a sense of order by eliminating clutter and distractions. So, we made the strategic choice to leverage the versatility of pictograms instead of relying on photography. These pictograms became the narrators of the message, injecting an element of playfulness that was traditionally absent from the world of 'taxes'. The outcome was a vibrant visual language that not only captivated the audience but also yielded positive results for the brand. What's remarkable is that even after many years, this iconography style still feels fresh and interesting and most importantly relevant.

Icons and pictograms can be used for various purposes, from signage to user interfaces. What are some common challenges you face in adapting your designs to different applications, and how do you address them?

One of the most critical practical challenges when working with pictograms and icons is ensuring readability. Whether the ultimate destination is print or digital, we often encounter issues such as resolution, which can significantly affect the complexity of the design. Furthermore, factors like the viewer's distance from the design or the context in which it will be experienced in physical space can steer the design in a particular direction. To address these challenges, I rely on a process of testing and trial. There's no substitute for getting hands-on and witnessing my work in the physical world, which involves creating mockups and props or conducting user testing for digital content. You can get a valuable amount of information and valuable feedback that is instrumental in refining the overall design.

For aspiring designers looking to integrate pictogram and icon design into their work, what advice would you give them? Are there key skills or practices they should prioritise in their journey?

It might be considered an unpopular opinion, but my advice is to carefully consider the use of icons and pictograms only when there's a genuine need for them. In recent years, I've observed a disproportionate use of iconography primarily for aesthetics rather than functionality. From my perspective, icons should be employed to represent a concept or an idea in situations where using words is impractical, often due to constraints like limited time or available space. I always encourage my collaborators and clients to use iconography with clear meaning and purpose. The best way to learn and gain more experience is through practice and testing.

However, I also recommend studying the work of influential designers such as Massimo Vignelli, Bob Noorda, and Paul Rand, as they were first to deal with the need for iconography and their early work can provide valuable lessons and insights for anyone working in this field. ●

☺ IN MY CREATIVE PROCESS, I HAVE A STRONG DESIRE TO GAIN A DEEP UNDERSTANDING OF MY AUDIENCE, TO WALK IN THEIR SHOES, GRASP THEIR SUBTLETIES, AND COMPREHEND THEIR INTERACTIONS WITH THE WORLD ☺

BIGGER

⊗ MICHELE VERZE
→ micheleverze.com

'Bigger' is an iconic takeaway
joint in the city centre of Verona,
northern Italy. Popular with university
students and known for its quality
products made from locally sourced
ingredients and meats, Bigger has
grown its fan base exponentially over
the years. So, when Bigger decided to
open a brand new restaurant, Michele
Verze was looking to build an identity
characterised by the playfulness
and fun of the employees, product
and customers. ●

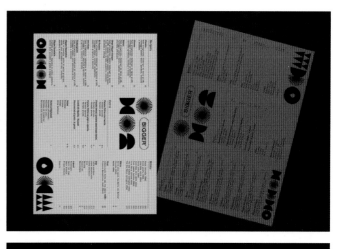

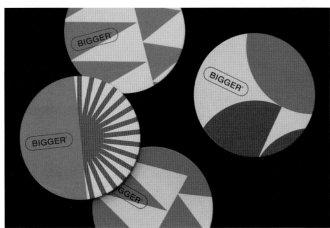

MICHELE VERZE WAS LOOKING TO BUILD AN IDENTITY
CHARACTERISED BY THE PLAYFULNESS AND FUN
OF THE EMPLOYEES, PRODUCT AND CUSTOMERS. ●

You say cheese. I say Asiago.

Big burgers con i migliori ingredienti tipici locali.

BIGGER®

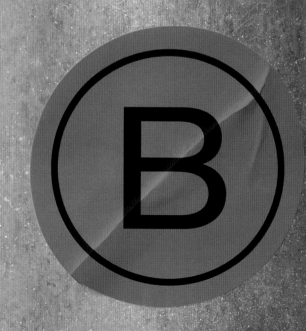

THE LAB COFFEE & CO.

HDU²³ LAB
→ hdu23lab.com

The Lab Coffee & Co. is a cafe that focuses on coffee taste testing and experience. To prioritise the experience of coffee itself, HDU²³ LAB designed a series of graphics for coffee brewing, taste and smell. They also redesigned the logo and changed the name of the brand simultaneously. ●

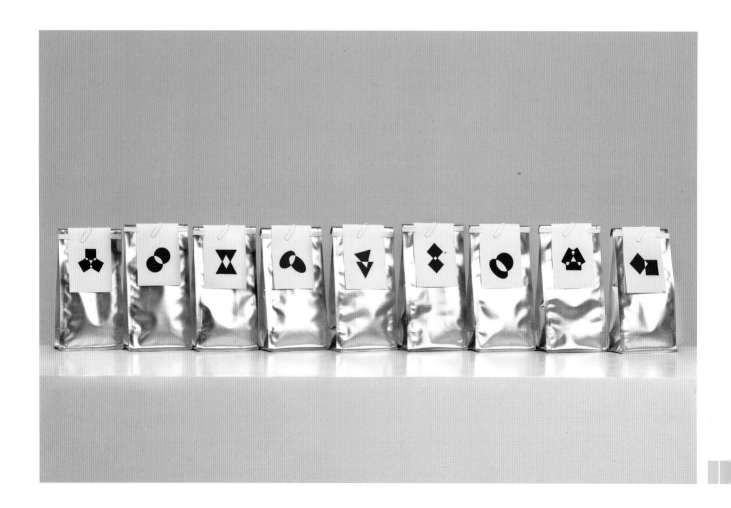

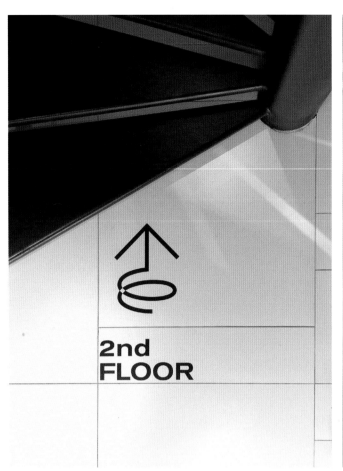

2nd
FLOOR

VIP
ROOM

THE
COFFEE
LAB

咖啡实验室内部墙面使用大
面积毛毡，其温和的触感语言
与抛光过的石材形成鲜明
对比，极富戏剧性。

THE WALL IS COVERED ALL
BY FELT. THE SOFT TACTILE
LANGUAGE OF FELT FORMS
A SHARP CONTRAST WITH
THE SMOOTH STONE OF THE
BAR, WHICH IS EXTREMELY
DRAMATIC.

HERMANOS
COLOMBIAN
COFFEE ROASTERS

✿ Fellow
→ fellowstudio.com

Hermanos Colombian Coffee Roasters wanted to amplify their founders' compelling narrative that their dedicated consumers have grown to adore, showcasing their dedication to quality and their passion and knowledge for specialty coffee. This led to the refinement of the pictogram, becoming a mark of authenticity and authorship. ●

DAYDREAM

✕ HDU²³ LAB
→ hdu23lab.com

'Daydream' is the theme of Spring 2021 for The Scientist Coffee. This season's new product is characterised by the fragrance of violet flowers. The visual identity design outlined the five feelings of the theme Daydream in the form of hand drawings, and a hand-drawn typeface was designed based on the skeleton of sans serif, which is intended to create a casual Spring mood for consumers and to echo the product's taste. ●

194

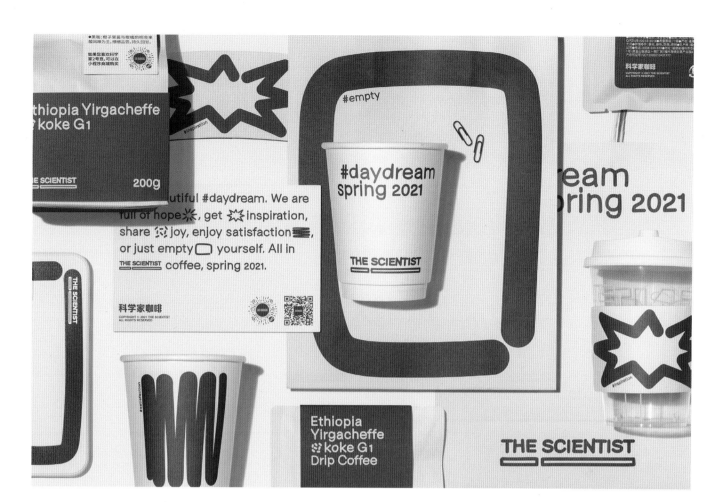

It's a beautiful #daydream. We are full of hope, get inspiration, share 😊 joy, enjoy satisfaction≡, or just empty ▭ yourself. All in THE SCIENTIST coffee, spring 2021.

科学家咖啡

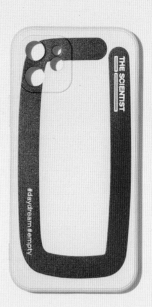

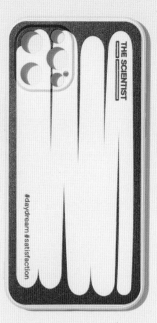

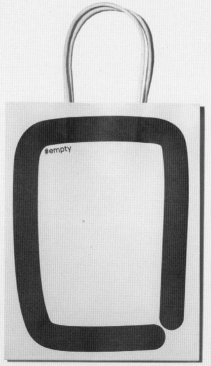

O'CARE

⊗ MADE
→ made-studio.ru

Naming, logo and package design for a new cosmetic brand that specialises in alginate facial masks. O'care makes 20 types of colourful masks, based on different ingredients, with young women as its prime target audience. MADE used a classic serif font for the logo and mixed it with a simple, modern identity, with simplified geometric icons symbolising mask ingredients. MADE were going for a design that can be easily understood by an everyday audience in a retail setting. ●

© 2024 Counter-Print
counter-print.co.uk
info@counter-print.co.uk

British Library cataloguing-in-publication
data: A catalogue of this book can be
found in the British Library.

First published in the United Kingdom
in 2024.

Edited and produced by Counter-Print.

Design: Counter-Print
Typeface: Studio Feixen Sans
Printing and Binding: 1010 Printing
International Limited, China
ISBN: 978-1-915392-11-4

200